Learn to Drive in 24 Hours

Learn

to Drive in 24 Hours

R H McCready

foulsham
London   New York   Toronto   Sydney

foulsham
The Publishing House, Bennetts Close,
Cippenham, Berkshire, SL1 5AP, England.

While every effort has been made to ensure the accuracy
of all the information contained within this book,
neither the author nor the publisher can be liable for any errors.
In particular, since laws change from time to time it is vital
that each individual should check relevant legal
details for themselves.

ISBN 0-572-02226-3

Design, page output and illustration by Barrie Carr
Cover design by Slatter-Anderson,
Printed in Great Britain by Cox & Wyman, Reading, Berkshire

Contents

Introduction

As any driving instructor will tell you, the safest and surest way to learn how to drive is to organise lessons so that you can work through from the basic exercises in car control to the most complex traffic situations, at your own pace and in a sequence that introduces you to the various problems as you feel able to cope with them.

Unfortunately, it would be impossible to arrange lessons in a book, in a sequence that will suit everybody because most people will be limited to learning within an area reasonably close to where they live and facilities vary from one place to another. One purpose of this book, however, is to show you how a series of lessons can be put together in a positive and progressive way so that each lesson can be productively spent working on problems that are relevant to an individual's own level of expertise.

This course is ideally suited to someone learning in the suburbs of a large town or city where there is access, in one direction, to faster roads leading out into the country and, in the other, to more congested streets and one way systems typical of most town centres. The lessons are arranged in a sequence that introduces you to the basic control of the car on quiet residential streets with simple junctions and shows you how you can progress in enjoyable and easy stages to more complex areas so that, at the end of the course, you should feel able to deal confidently with any type of road or traffic situation without the help of an instructor.

Even if you do not have the facilities in your area to cover every problem or situation, this book will allow you to get some idea of how many different types of road, junction, or traffic situation there are, and the various exercises will enable you to arrange a programme best suited to your needs.

Each lesson should be organised so as to give yourself a specific objective each time you drive, so that at the end of each lesson you feel that you have made progress in some way. At the very least you should have fully understood the rules, techniques, and procedures required; at best you should feel confident of tackling the same exercise successfully every time.

To that end you should plan your routes carefully in advance, so that you will be able to concentrate fully on the relevant problem with the minimum of distraction. It is normally best to use a route that takes you back to where you started so that you can repeat the exercise as often as required.

The new theory test

From July 1996 the Highway Code section of the test will be replaced by a separate written exam. For the following six months you will be allowed to do the two driving tests in any order but from January 1997 you will need to pass the written exam first and then you will have two years to pass the practical. The new test will be available in various languages, and arrangements will be made for people with special needs.

As well as the Highway Code, the theory test will cover such things as alertness, weather conditions, vehicle handling, accidents, motorways and the environment. The questions are multiple choice. Usually you will have to pick one from four suggested answers, though some questions may ask for more than one choice from more than four answers. Although many people fear exams, this theory test is no more complicated than the original Highway Code test. Its aim is to help you increase your overall understanding of the basic principles of driving as well as testing your knowledge of the Highway Code. With this book you will learn to be a skillful driver and develop a good driver attitude. Once you have these skills, passing the theory test should follow naturally. To help you get the feel of a written test, some multiple choice questions are included at the end of this book.

Environment

Where you learn to drive will make an enormous difference to what you learn, how quickly you learn, and most importantly, how much you enjoy learning.

The type of road you drive on, the amount of traffic, and the complexity of the problems encountered, need to be organised so that you can be introduced to them as and when you are ready. You could, of

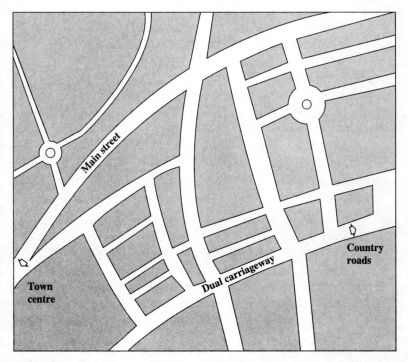

course, simply go for a drive and see what crops up, but in most cases this will only lead to tensions, arguments, and possibly accidents.

The ideal environment for learning should centre on a quiet area where you have plenty of room to relax and carry out basic control exercises in the first few lessons, but from where you have easy access to different types of junctions, busier or faster roads, and more complex traffic situations.

The area in the map is typical of most towns. It centres on the residential suburbs where roads are fairly wide and the traffic is light – an environment ideally suited to beginners. It is bordered on one side by a main road where the traffic is heavier, on the other by a dual carriageway with fast moving traffic. The dual carriageway leads to the country roads, while the main road leads into the centre of town with its busy streets and one way system.

This book shows how such an environment can be used to build up a sequence of lessons, adding on or omitting the various roads, junctions, and traffic conditions as required.

TOWN CENTRE

MAIN STREET

DUAL CARRIAGEWAY

COUNTRY ROADS

Licence

You must have a valid provisional licence. If you don't have one you can get an application form from any post office or driving school.

Health

If you suffer from an illness or disability you must declare it on the application form if its affects are expected to last for more than three months, or if you suffer from an ailment that may recur (such as epilepsy).

Eyesight

You must be able to read a number plate at a distance of 20.5 metres (67 feet or about 5-6 car lengths). If you need to wear glasses to read the number plate you must also wear them to drive.

Car

If you are learning to drive in your own car, or a car belonging to a relative or friend, you must make sure that it is properly taxed, insured (check that the insurance covers you as a learner), and roadworthy (if over 3 years old it should have an MOT certificate) and that you have L-plates facing to the front and rear. You must also be accompanied by a fully qualified driver who is at least 21 years old and who has held a full licence for that type of vehicle for 3 years or more.

Driving School

This book helps you learn to drive with a relative or friend, but you should consider getting lessons from a professional too. Most driving schools will provide you with a good quality car equipped with dual controls, and an instructor who can help you to avoid the hazards of learning to drive while at the same time showing you the correct procedures and techniques to follow.

Literature

It doesn't matter how good the instructor may be; ultimately it's up to you how much you understand and how quickly you learn. There are lots of books you can buy at any bookshop or borrow from the library which explain the basics of driving. Obviously you must learn your Highway Code, and there are also books to help with this. There is no reason why you should not know how to drive in theory even before you sit in the driver's seat for the first time. Foulsham, who publish this book, also have a range of other books on driving and the Highway Code. You could save yourself a lot of time and money – so get reading!

Settling down
Controls
Starting and stopping

As a beginner, the first lesson is always the most nerve-wracking, mainly because you don't know what to expect or whether you will be able to cope. In fact the first lesson is the most straightforward and probably the only one that every instructor does in more or less the same way.

You should be driven to a quiet residential area where there is very little traffic and you can learn the basics of driving in safety. Once there, your instructor can get you settled down in the driving seat and familiarise you with the car by giving you a brief explanation of the controls.

You can later be shown the material in lesson 2, which will let you deal with the junctions you may meet; or, if you have a long and uninterrupted road, you may just wish to get the starting and stopping right. Either way, you will drive the car slowly, starting and stopping frequently.

By the end of the lesson you should be able to:

1. remember the checks to be made when you get into the car;
2. know what the six basic controls are and briefly what they do;
3. understand how to start and stop uphill, downhill, and on the level.

Settling down

Every time you get into the driving seat of the car there are five checks you should make before setting off.

Doors

Check your doors are properly shut. If you have a four door car check the back doors as well, particularly if you are carrying young children or elderly passengers.

Seat

Adjust the base of the seat so that you can control the foot pedals comfortably. You should be able to rest your feet on the floor behind the pedals and use little more than an ankle movement to operate the controls.

Steering

On some cars you can adjust the rake of the steering wheel. On others you can adjust the back of the seat. With your shoulders resting comfortably against the back of the seat you should be able to reach the steering wheel, the gear lever, and the main switches on the dashboard without having to stretch and without feeling uncomfortably bunched up.

Seat belt

The law demands that you must wear a seat belt at all times while driving, except while carrying out a manoeuvre involving reverse. You are only exempt if you hold a medical exemption certificate from your doctor or if you are driving a local delivery vehicle such as milk float.

Mirrors

Adjust the driver's mirror and the door mirrors so as to give yourself the best possible view of the road behind. The driver's mirror should be adjusted so that you can see a reflection of the road behind without moving your head from a normal driving position. The door mirrors should be adjusted so that you can see a little of your own car as well as the road behind; then you can see where other drivers are in relation to your own car. Many door mirrors are convex so that they give a wide angled view, but that will make other vehicles seem further away than they really are.

Foot controls

Accelerator

Often called the gas pedal by instructors, the accelerator is operated with your right foot. The more you press the pedal the faster the engine goes. The main difficulty is in controlling the pressure on the pedal, particularly when you are trying to control the clutch or steering at the same time.

Brake

Also worked with your right foot, the brake acts hydraulically on all four wheels simultaneously. Like the accelerator the main difficulty is to feel how much pressure is needed to slow the car, particularly if you are trying to change gear at the same time.

Clutch

Worked with your left foot, the clutch pedal is pressed down to temporarily separate the engine from the gearbox and wheels, thus allowing you to change gear or stop the car without stopping the engine. It does this by separating two plates that are normally pressed together by springs. Bringing the clutch up after selecting a gear allows the spinning plate which is connected to the engine to press against the plate that is connected to the gearbox, and so turn the wheels. This action must be done carefully if a smooth start or gear change is to be made, since the clutch plates will normally be turning at different rates while separated. The point at which the clutch plates just make contact, so that only part of the engine's power is transmitted to the wheels, is called the BITING POINT.

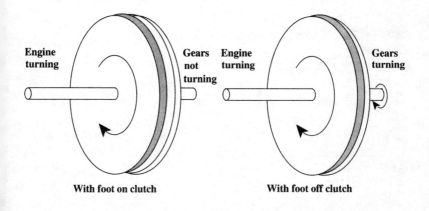

Engine turning   Gears not turning   Engine turning   Gears turning

With foot on clutch   **With foot off clutch**

Hand controls

Gears

Most cars have four forward gears and a reverse gear, although many are also equipped with a fifth gear. The usual arrangement is that the gears are laid out in an 'H' pattern, with reverse to one side.

The gears are used to vary the ratio between engine speed and car speed. In simple terms this means that if the engine is kept at the optimum speed while the car speed varies, the car will always feel responsive to acceleration and deceleration. Too high or too low an engine speed will diminish this responsiveness and therefore also the amount of control you have over the car. For instance, if you tried to do 20 mph in fourth gear the engine would be going too slow to deliver much power. In second or third gear it could turn faster, at a speed where it works better. Part of the skill of driving lies in being able to select the most appropriate gear to suit your speed or circumstances.

Handbrake

Usually positioned on the floor between the front seats but sometimes found under the dashboard or to the right of the driver's seat, the handbrake is used to hold the car steady once you have stopped. It should not be used to stop the car. To apply the handbrake, press the button on the end, pull the lever up tightly, and release the button. To release, pull the lever up, press the button in, and put the lever to the floor.

Steering wheel

Although the reason for having a steering wheel is obvious, the approved technique for turning the wheel may be less so. While driving in a straight line your hands should be kept on the wheel in a ten-to-two position as on a clock face, or slightly lower if you prefer in a quarter-to-three position.When turning a corner you should pass the wheel around in a push-pull movement so that your hands do not cross the top or bottom of the wheel.

Starting on level ground

It would be difficult to imagine anyone learning to drive without their first practical lesson being in starting and stopping. As with many other driving exercises, these can be carried out safely and under control each time by following the correct sequence of actions. These are as follows.

Preparation
1. Clutch down.
2. Select first gear.
3. Put your foot lightly on the accelerator. (About 1500–2000 rpm if your car is fitted with a tachometer.)
4. Bring the clutch up to the biting point (so that the car almost starts to move forward) and hold it steady.

Observation
1. Check the mirror.
2. Check the blind spot (by turning around to look over your right shoulder).
3. Indicate to the right.

Manoeuvre
1. Release the handbrake.
2. Accelerate and bring the clutch up fully.
3. Switch off the indicator if it does not switch itself off.

Starting uphill

Although the sequence of actions is much the same as when starting on level ground, the main difficulty is usually in finding the biting point on the clutch before releasing the handbrake. If you don't bring the clutch up far enough the car will roll backward, but if you bring the clutch up too far the engine will stall or the car will surge forward as soon as the handbrake is released.

Preparation
1. Clutch down.
2. Select first gear.

3. Put your foot lightly on the accelerator (2000–2500 rpm if your car is fitted with a tachometer).
4. Bring the clutch up to the biting point and hold it steady. (You can usually feel the car pull gently against the brake.)
5. Release the handbrake.

Observation
1. Check your mirrors.
2. Check the blind spot (look around over your right shoulder).
3. Indicate to the right.

Manoeuvre
1. Bring the clutch up very slightly and hold it steady for a few seconds whilst the car moves forward.
2. Accelerate and bring the clutch up completely.
3. Make sure the indicator is off.

Starting downhill

Starting downhill is very simple because the car will roll forward as soon as you release the handbrake. Because of this you need less power to accelerate so you can use second gear instead of first in many cases, particularly if the hill is very steep. Procedures are similar to other starts.

Preparation
1. Clutch down.
2. Select first (or second) gear.
3. Apply the footbrake.
4. Release the handbrake.

Observation
1. Check the mirrors.
2. Check the blind spot (over your right shoulder).
3. Indicate to the right.

Manoeuvre
1. Release the footbrake.

2. Release the clutch and accelerate.
3. Check that the indicator has switched off.

It might be useful to know if you have difficulty starting your engine (i.e. if your battery is flat) that you could 'bump start' your car by following the same actions as above. As long as the ignition is switched on, the engine should start as soon as the clutch is lifted.

Stopping (on the left)

You will find that stopping the car requires the same sequence of actions whether you are stopping uphill, downhill, or on level ground. The only difference is the obvious one – that you will have to brake harder when driving downhill than you will when driving uphill. The main difficulty is in regulating the pressure on the brake pedal correctly so that you do not stop abruptly.

1. Check the mirror.
2. Indicate to the left.
3. Ease off the accelerator and steer to the left.
4. Brake as necessary to slow the car down.
5. Push the clutch down just before you stop.
6. Let the car roll to a gentle halt.
7. Pull the handbrake up firmly.
8. Select neutral.
9. Cancel the indicator.
10. Take your feet off the pedals.

Starting and stopping with an automatic gearbox

In a car fitted with an automatic gearbox, starting and stopping is a very simple process, and it doesn't make any difference whether you are starting on a hill or on level ground. Once 'Drive' is selected, an automatic car will not roll backwards, even on the steepest hill and, unlike a manual car, it is quite difficult to stall the engine.

Starting

Preparation
1. Footbrake on.
2. Select 'Drive'.
3. Release the handbrake.

Observation
1. Check the mirror.
2. Check the blind spot.
3. Indicate to the right.

Manoeuvre
1. Release the footbrake.
2. Press the accelerator.

Stopping on the left

1. Check the mirror.
2. Signal to the left.
3. Ease off the accelerator and steer to the left.
4. Gently brake to a halt.
5. Pull the handbrake up fully.
6. Select neutral.
7. Cancel the indicator.

Lesson 2

Second gear
T-Junctions

If you have not run straight on from lesson 1, you should start in the same area, and spend some time practising what you learnt before. You then go on to learn how to change from first to second gear, and how to cope with simple T-junctions.

As before, you will drive slowly. You will probably be confined to a fairly small area so that you will be able to learn to steer right and left without having too much other traffic to worry about.

By the end of the lesson you should:

1. have some idea about how and when to change from first to second gear;
2. be clear about your positioning and priorities at a T-junction.

Changing from first to second gear

Once you have understood how to start and stop in first gear you will often find it easier to drive slowly using second gear, even at a very early stage. If, like many people, you are having difficulty controlling the steering, second gear will drive the car along at a steadier pace than first, allowing you to feel more easily which way the wheels are pointing.

Start off as usual in first gear.
Accelerate to around 10 or 15 mph.
Clutch down.
Off the accelerator.
Change from first to second gear.
Clutch up smoothly.
Put your foot back on the accelerator.

When changing down you may need to increase the accelerator a little, rather than lowering it, for a smooth change.

Be careful when you press the clutch while going downhill; you may actually speed up.

Routine exercises should give you a chance to understand how, when, and why to change up to second gear. Start off with your instructor telling you exactly how and when to change up or down gear. After a few attempts try to judge for yourself when to change gear. You can stop in second gear, or whatever other gear you happen to be in.

T-Junctions

It is fairly obvious why a T-junction is so called; it is where two roads meet at right angles to form a 'T'.

Usually the road forming the crossbar of the 'T' is the major road and the stalk of the 'T' the minor road. Traffic emerging from the minor road must give priority to traffic on the major road, stopping if necessary.

This priority can be altered or emphasised by using 'Stop' signs or traffic lights but more commonly by 'Give Way' lines – broken white lines painted across the end of the minor road and often accompanied by an inverted triangular 'Give Way' sign at the roadside.

As with any manoeuvre, you must first check in your mirror to make

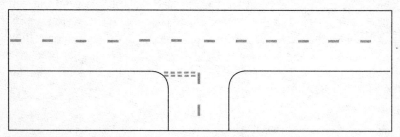

sure it's safe, and signal if there is anyone else around.

The basic points of most importance to the driver concern the rules of priority and positioning.

1.   When turning left into the minor road you would normally keep

close to the left hand side of the road, stopping only if there are pedestrians crossing the road you want to enter or if your path is obstructed.

2. Turning left into the major road you would also keep to the left, but you might have to stop to check that the major road is clear before continuing.

3. Turning right into the major road you would normally position parallel and close to the centre of the road, once again stopping if necessary to check that the major road is clear before continuing.

4. Turning right into the minor road requires a similar position parallel and close to the centre of the road, but you must stop and wait for traffic approaching you on the major road before continuing. Once again, you must wait for pedestrians crossing the road you want to enter.

Lesson 3

Steering problems
Clutch control problems
Crossroads
Zebra crossings

Again, you should go to the same area and practise what you have covered so far. If you have any problems you should try to solve them before moving on to the next exercises.

For the next couple of lessons you will need to add a few more roads to your now familiar beginners area – but not too many. A few more residential streets with crossroads as well as T-junctions; perhaps a parade of shops with a few pedestrians, a bit of traffic and a zebra crossing is enough to provide interest without being alarming, and more importantly without distracting you from the main purpose of the lessons.

By the end of the lesson, in addition to feeling more confident about performing the basic skills learnt in lessons 1 and 2, you should:

1. know the rules concerning positioning and priorities at crossroads;
2. be clear about the rules concerning zebra crossings.

Steering problems

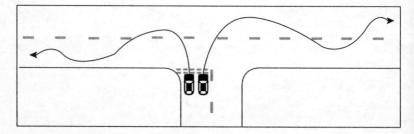

The diagrams show the most common problems while cornering. Instead of following an accurate course, the car is steered in a wide circle. One moment you are in danger of hitting the kerb, the next you are crossing the centre line and endangering other traffic. The usual causes are as follows.

1. Aiming the car instead of the wheels

In the left turn illustrated below, you can see that if the steering is rotated to the left and held in that position the car will follow a regular curve, but the front of the car will always be heading in a different direction to the wheels.

The wheels are pointing along the edge of the road long before the car comes parallel. Half way around the corner a person looking at the bonnet of the car would be tempted to turn further to the left, whereas a driver correctly visualising the path taken by the wheels would be starting to straighten up.

2. Poor steering technique

If you don't use full continuous movements to turn the wheel, the steering will be slow and inaccurate. The usual mistakes are to use a lot of short, choppy movements which take a lot of work but produce very little turning; or to use a full movement, but only pulling down two or three times on the same side, rather than pushing up with one hand and pulling down with the other equally.

3. Poor clutch control

If you have stopped at a junction, the car should not surge forward when you start off again. Practice the clutch control exercise so that you can hold the clutch steady at the biting point while steering. In slow manoeuvres the power is controlled with your accelerator but the speed is controlled with your clutch.

4. Wrong line of approach

You need to visualise your proposed line through the corner and stick to it. For example, when turning left out of a minor road, a common mistake is to approach and stop in a straight line, rather than curving to the left with the kerb. In other words, the car has been aimed only to the end of the road instead of along an imaginary line that continues around the corner.

5. Taking the corner at the wrong speed

The mistake is to approach too fast so that you end up braking as you turn the corner. This will cause the car to understeer and go wide. The car should be at the correct speed and in the correct gear before you reach the corner. The problem may lie in poor use of deceleration or braking, or a lack of co-ordination in changing gear while braking. Make sure the clutch is up when you are turning the corner.

6. Being distracted by other people

You cannot possibly expect to keep the car on an accurate course if you are looking in the wrong direction. Make sure that you clearly understand who has priority at any junction and that you know where to stop if necessary. You must watch other road users but even if there are a lot of vehicles or pedestrians you should still concentrate mainly on your own proposed route, looking at the layout of the road, the road signs, and the white lines, and responding to them and to obstructions in your path.

7. Being distracted by your own controls

Looking down at the controls will cause steering inaccuracies, especially when changing gear during the early stages of your driving, but with practice you should be able to find and use all the main controls by touch alone. If you are unsure of where the minor controls are (such as lights or wipers) you should stop at the roadside instead of experimenting while on the move.

Clutch control problems

Poor clutch control is one of those problems that is immediately apparent to anybody. Without good control you cannot start off smoothly; you roll back on hills, stall frequently, change gear roughly, and generally find manoeuvres like reversing or turning the car around much more difficult.

Like everything else, clutch control will improve with practice. The following exercises might be helpful.

1. Stop on a hill (going up); select first gear; bring the clutch up to the biting point; release the handbrake and hold the car stationary. The car shouldn't roll back or forward, and the engine speed should be kept steady so that it's not roaring on one hand, or in danger of stalling on the other. You should make sure that you keep both heels on the floor so that your feet are properly supported, and you should feel comfortable and relaxed.

2. As a second part of this exercise, bring the clutch up very slightly so that the car moves slowly forward. Move about a car length and then squeeze the clutch down again to the biting point and hold the car steady. Now press the clutch down a fraction so that the car rolls back a car length and once again find the biting point and hold the car steady.

3. Facing downhill, try the same exercises using reverse gear. Many people find this confusing at first, but it might help you to understand the clutch better.

4. On level ground move forward at an absolute snail's pace with the engine at idling speed. Now increase the pressure on the accelerator gradually (to 2000–3000 rpm) but keep the clutch at biting point by pushing it in further, so that your speed never rises above snail's pace. You should be able to increase or decrease power at will without any change in speed.

5. The co-ordination needed for clutch control will always be more difficult when you also have to steer, as you do on most manoeuvres. As a simple exercise, stop about a car length behind a parked vehicle and then drive around it at a snail's pace to stop again a car length in front. This could be done uphill or on the level. Of course, uphill is much harder.

Crossroads

A crossroads is simply a junction where one road crosses another, usually at right angles. The rules concerning positioning and priority are similar to those at a T-junction if slightly more complex. Traffic priority can be altered or emphasised by using 'Stop' signs or traffic lights, but the basic junction is most commonly controlled by 'Give Way' signs.

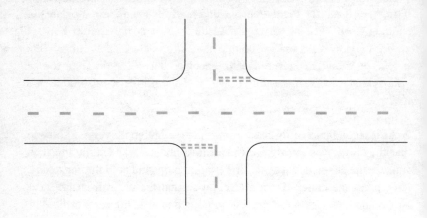

Positioning

If you are turning left from any direction, you position close to the left hand side of the road.

If you are turning right from any direction, you approach along a path that is both close and parallel to the centre line. Avoid cutting the corner; come far enough forward to see along the new road before you turn into it. If you are going straight ahead from any direction you would normally keep to the normal driving position on the left.

Priorities

Cars emerging from the minor roads, whether going right, left, or straight ahead, have to stop for traffic on the major road to pass, before continuing.

Any traffic on the major road should therefore be able to continue uninterrupted if it is going straight ahead or left.

Any traffic turning right from any direction must wait for cars approaching from the opposite direction to pass before turning. This can be a problem if the oncoming traffic also wants to turn right. No one has outright priority, and the rules to follow (118 and 119 in the Highway Code) say that you should pass around behind each other if that is practical, or in front of each other if that is more practical. The correct course of action depends on the size and layout of the junction and on road markings.

Zebra crossings

The zebra crossing gets its name because it consists of black and white stripes painted across the road. Even the constantly flashing amber lights at both ends of the crossing – called Belisha beacons – are mounted on black and white striped poles. The main rules concerning zebra crossings are as follows.

1. If there are any pedestrians waiting to cross the road you should stop and let them cross, even if they have not yet set foot on the crossing.

2. Once the pedestrian has stepped on to the crossing you are obliged by law to give way and let them cross.

3. A traffic island in the middle of the crossing effectively divides it in two. You should treat each half as a separate crossing, giving way to those pedestrians on your half of the road.

4. You are not allowed to park or overtake on the approaches to the crossing in the area marked by zig-zag lines.

5. Even if you cannot see any pedestrians you should make a habit of checking your mirror and both sides of the crossing as you approach, slowing if necessary.

Lesson 4

Use of third gear
Explanation of gears

The main objective of this lesson is to teach you how to use third gear and to give you an understanding of when and why you should change from one gear to another. As before you should start with a review of what you have learnt so far, so that you can settle down.

By the end of this lesson you should:

1. understand how, when, and why you should change gear;
2. feel comfortable changing to and from third gear.

Adding on a third gear

As with the change from first to second gear the concern here should be how, when, and why to change up and down between second and third gear. Normally the change up from second to third presents fewer problems than changing back down again, since the change down often has to be done at the right time, within a limited road space, and possibly while adjusting the speed as well.

Changing up from second to third gear

Start off as usual in first gear.
Accelerate up into second gear.
Speed up a bit more (20–25 mph).
Clutch down, and at the same time:
Ease off the accelerator.
Change up to third gear.
Bring the clutch up smoothly again.
Put your foot back on the accelerator.

Changing down from third to second gear

Take your foot off the accelerator.
Clutch down, and at the same time:
Apply a little pressure to the accelerator, or:
brake a little.
Change from third to second gear.
Bring the clutch smoothly up again.

It should be noted that, when changing down your right foot would be controlling the speed, so depending on whether you want to speed up, slow down or maintain a steady speed, your right foot might be controlling the accelerator or brake as necessary throughout the gear change. The brake is better when slowing, or at slower speeds.

Understanding gears

The gearbox on your car is used to alter the ratio between engine speed and car speed. The graph below might help to explain.

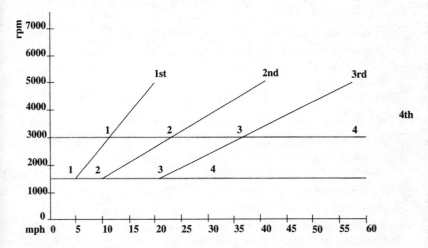

When you switch on the engine it will tick over at 800 rpm. At this speed it is producing very little power.

The 'power band' will vary from one engine to another. In my example the engine will be at its most efficient between 1500 and 3000 rpm. To start off you would therefore select first gear and put your foot on the accelerator to raise the engine speed to around 1500 rpm. This would give you enough power to pull the car forward.

You could accelerate in first gear to about 15 mph, but at this speed the engine will be starting to over-rev as it passes 3000 rpm. To stay within the power band you would have to change up to second gear. Second gear will take you to about 25 mph before the engine once again begins to over-rev and third gear is needed. Third gear in turn will allow you to accelerate up to 40 mph before you need to use fourth gear.

All these figures are interesting if your car is fitted with a tachometer as well as a speedometer, but in practice you wouldn't watch these instruments anyway. Instead you would feel and hear the response of the engine. If your engine speed drops below 1500 rpm you will feel the engine begin to chug and rattle. It will not be pulling the car forward smoothly and efficiently and you will need to change down a gear.

On the other hand, if the engine speed rises above 3000 rpm it will start to sound excessively noisy and will become progressively inefficient, so you will need to change up to the next higher gear.

By listening to the engine and feeling its response you should be able to not only accelerate and decelerate smoothly, but also to feel whether you are selecting the best gear for the conditions. For example, if you are driving uphill at 30 mph you might feel that third gear is most appropriate since it provides you with the optimum power, but on level ground at 30 mph you need less power to maintain a steady speed, so fourth gear would be more appropriate, quieter and more economical since the engine is not running so fast.

When slowing down it should be noted that, although it is quite acceptable to stop in any gear, the engine should be used to help deceleration, particularly in slippery conditions where it would be unwise to brake too heavily.

As with acceleration, the engine is best used for this purpose by keeping within the power band. In the graph, for example, fourth gear falls below 1500 rpm at 30 mph, so at this speed you would change down to third gear to make best use of engine braking. Like acceleration this is largely a matter of listening to and feeling the response of the engine, but since the timing of the gear change must coincide more accurately with the speed of the car, which must in turn fit in with the road or traffic situation, correctly made down changes present greater difficulty and need constant practice.

In good conditions you do not need to change down through the gears when you know you are going to stop, but you do need to when you may have to speed up again without stopping, such as at a 'Give Way' sign.

Exercises for understanding gears

You should carry out a few simple exercises designed to help you to understand not only how, but also when and why to change gear.

1. Drive a suitable short route with your instructor telling you exactly when to change up and down gears. If you drive the same route two or three times so that you are familiar with where you are going you will find it easier to concentrate on the gear changes. Then drive the same route while trying to judge for yourself when to change gear.

2. Experiment with the gears so that you can better understand why one gear is more suitable than another in various situations. I have listed a few experiments below that you can try in third gear.

a) Try starting off in third gear instead of first.
b) Stop in third gear (note that this is often acceptable).
c) At slow speed turn into a side road in third gear.
d) Accelerate and decelerate between 10 and 30 mph in third gear.
e) Hold a steady 15 mph in third gear going up and down hill.

In each case you should compare the amount of control with that in first or second gear. Note in particular the response when you accelerate or decelerate in each gear, and the effect this has on the amount of control you have over speed and steering.

Automatic gears

In a car fitted with a manual gearbox, the power from the engine is transmitted through a clutch and gearbox to the wheels. The gears are selected at the discretion of the driver, and the clutch must be used skillfully to start, stop, and change gear smoothly. Many people take pride in their ability to use the clutch and gears effectively, but many more find it a tedious chore to be avoided if possible, or a great difficulty. A disabled person might find it impossible.

In a car fitted with an automatic transmission, the need for any skill with clutch and gears is removed. There is no clutch pedal and the gearbox automatically selects higher and lower gears as the car is driven faster or slower. The driver has only two pedals, an accelerator and a brake, with which to start, stop, and control the speed. In place of the gear lever is a selector.

Although gearboxes will vary slightly from one make of car to another, the basic functions of the selector are very similar.

Park (P)

Placing the selector in the 'Park' position has a similar effect to leaving a manual gearbox in a gear when you switch off the engine. It locks up the gearbox so that there is no danger of the car rolling downhill. It should therefore be used in addition to the handbrake when you leave the car.

Reverse (R)

You would, of course, move the selector to the reverse position when you want to go backwards, but be careful that you put your foot on the footbrake before selecting the gear; otherwise the car could start to move back before you are ready.

Neutral (N)

You should select neutral before you switch on the engine. As with a manual gearbox, neutral means that no gear is selected and so there is no danger of the car driving back or forward accidentally when you switch the engine on. You will also reduce wear on the transmission if you select neutral when you are stopped for a long time with the engine running.

Manual positions (1), (2), (3)

These 'Manual Hold' positions override the automatic capability of the gearbox. As with a manual gearbox you select the gear most suited to your need. You might use this facility when towing at slower speeds, when engine braking is required, or in any situation where more control over the gears would be an advantage, such as in icy conditions.

Drive (D)

To take full advantage of the automatic capabilities of the gearbox you would select 'Drive'. With the selector in this position you can start, stop and control the speed simply by using the accelerator and foot-brake. Press the footbrake when selecting 'Drive' to avoid any unintentional movement, and then press the accelerator to drive forward. As you speed up and slow down, the gearbox will automatically select the most appropriate gear. To slow down or stop, simply press the foot-brake.

Exercises for understanding automatic gears

In a manual car it is essential that you understand the gears so that you can select the correct gear to suit the speed and conditions. In an automatic, this is not so important because, once you select 'Drive', the gearbox will automatically select the correct gear. However, since most automatic cars are fitted with two or three manually selected gears as well, you should be aware of their functions and effect, so that you could use them if necessary. You should also be aware of 'kick-down' and its effect.

To feel the effects of 'kick-down':

a) accelerate smoothly up to 30 mph and then slow down again, listening to the engine and noting the gear changes;
b) then accelerate as quickly as possible up to 30 mph by pressing the accelerator flat to the floor for a few seconds, again noting the gear changes (or lack of them).

The heavy acceleration will bring in the 'kick-down' facility, where the gearbox automatically changes to a lower gear and holds that gear so that you can accelerate quickly.

To feel the effects of each manual overide:

a) on level ground, try starting off in each of the gears in turn, so that you can feel their effect on acceleration and deceleration;

b) then compare their effect while driving uphill or downhill;

c) select 'Drive' under the same conditions and again compare the effect.

Hopefully, by experimenting in this way, you will not only gain an insight into why an automatic car is fitted with manual gears, but you will also be able to make use of them if the need arises.

Lesson 5

Approaching junctions
Roundabouts
Traffic lights

This lesson begins, as usual, by allowing you time to settle down and practise the skills you have already covered, using the same roads as before. Once again you should try to overcome any problems before moving on to the next exercises.

Then the way to approach junctions can be formalised, before going on to other types of junction.

Once you have come to grips with any problems, you can expand your knowledge of basic junctions by adding a roundabout to your route. As with the other junctions, your instructor should explain the rules before asking you to put them into practice. Your first roundabout should be fairly clear of traffic.

When you come to traffic lights you may have to deal with a little more traffic, though you should still try to find a reasonably quiet place to start.

By the end of this lesson you should:

1. understand the proper procedure at roundabouts;
2. know the procedures and stopping distances approaching traffic lights.

Sequence approaching junctions

As with many other areas of driving, the approach to junctions will be carried out more safely and without omissions if all the necessary actions are done in the same sequence every time. Although there will be exceptions you should aim to follow the pattern below.

Mirrors

By checking your mirrors you will be better able to judge when to signal, how to position, and how quickly to slow down in relation to following traffic.

Signal

Indicate your intention early enough for other traffic to be able to react, but not so early as to be confusing. Don't, for instance, indicate right when there is another opening on the right before the one you want. Make sure you are indicating in the correct direction!

Position

Generally speaking you would position to the centre of the road to turn right or to the left if you are turning left.

Speed

Once you have positioned correctly you can slow down for the junction. The rate at which you slow will depend on how close you are to the junction, but you should try to slow at a rate that causes least disruption to following traffic.

Gear

Which gear you select will depend on the speed of the car and you might have to change more than once, but you should try to select the gear appropriate to your speed as you are slowing down.

Check

Where you check will depend on the type of junction you are approaching. For example, it would mean looking right and left if you are approaching Give Way lines, looking ahead for traffic and to the right for obstructions if you are turning right into a minor road, or simply looking left for obstructions if you are turning left into a side road. Look for cyclists and pedestrians.

Roundabouts

The main problem at a busy crossroads is that vehicles approaching and leaving the junction have to manoeuvre around or across each other's paths, with drivers often having to watch in two or three directions at the same time. A misjudgment or misunderstanding can lead to a collision or a hold-up.

Roundabouts were designed to alleviate this problem by channelling all vehicles into a small one way system running clockwise around an island in the middle of the junction. The rules of priority are thus simplified. All drivers on approach to the junction need only to look to their right and give priority to those already on the roundabout.

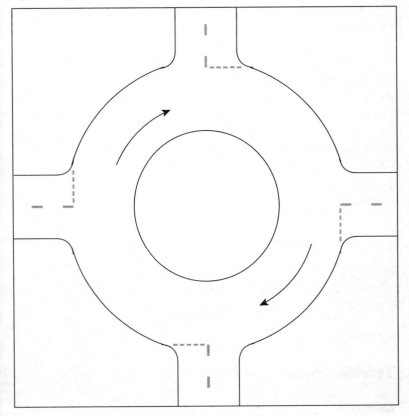

The rules most likely to cause confusion are those concerning positioning the car and signalling correctly.

Positioning

As with any junction you would normally keep to the left hand lane when turning left or going straight ahead and keep to the right hand lane, and close to the centre of the roundabout, when turning right ('right' means any exit that is more than halfway round). On the right turn, leave on a tangential course from the centre of the roundabout to the left hand side of the exit road.

Signals

On approach, signal as you would at a crossroads – right if you are turning right, left if you are turning left, and nothing if you are going straight ahead. Before leaving the roundabout, signal left as you pass the exit before the one you intend taking.

Like the crossroads, the signals on approach allow each driver to know the other's intended route while moving into the most appropriate lane or position. The exit signal, on the other hand, is of greatest benefit to drivers approaching the roundabout from other directions, since they will be better able to decide whether to stop or continue once they know which exit you are taking.

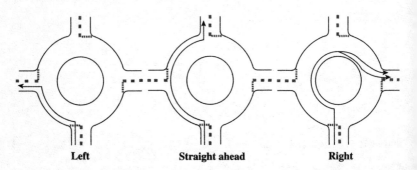

| Left | Straight ahead | Right |

Traffic lights

Red

Stop behind the stop line. Apply the handbrake so that there is no chance of the car rolling, and select neutral if you think the lights will be red for some time. This not only allows you to relax your feet for a few moments; it also minimises wear and tear to the clutch and gearbox.

Red and Amber

Get ready to move off but do not move until the green light shows and the road is clear.

Green

Go if the road is clear. You might have to wait for pedestrians crossing the road. Both of these situations apply if you have been waiting at the lights.

Approaching the green light at speed can be much more difficult. If the light changes as you approach you need to decide quickly whether it is safest to stop or continue.

Approaching the green light in slow-moving traffic can also be tricky. You need to be sure that you can get right across the junction without being forced to stop halfway.

At busier junctions a 'box junction' is often painted on the road to emphasise this rule. You may not move onto the area marked with yellow-criss-cross lines unless your exit road is clear.

Amber

Stop, unless you have already crossed the stop line or you are too close to the line to stop safely. Being able to judge when you can stop safely and when you are committed to passing the lights is a skill that must be developed.

Filter lights

On some traffic lights there are filter arrows which allow traffic turning right or left to continue while the main light stays red. Be careful not to get into a filter lane unless you intend turning in that direction.

Committal and stopping distances

Approaching traffic lights showing green can be a treacherous business.

The lights could change at any time, and the Highway Code tells you that if the lights change to amber you should stop unless you have already crossed the stop line or you are so close to it that to pull up would cause an accident. Many accidents have been caused by the driver misjudging the distance to the stop line.

If you are further away than you think, you will go through a red light and risk colliding with vehicles starting off from the right and left; if you are too close you will stop too quickly and following vehicles may crash in to the back of your car.

The problem can be alleviated by making practical use of the table of stopping distances in the Highway Code. As you approach the traffic lights you take note of any following vehicles, note your speed, then mark out a point before the lights that is roughly equivalent to the stopping distance (you don't want to do an emergency stop), beyond which you commit yourself to passing the lights even if they change.

For example, if you are travelling at 30 mph on a dry road surface with a vehicle following at a safe distance, your committal point would be a little under 23 metres (75 feet) from the lights. You mark out your point, which could be an imaginary line, a lamp post, or a parked car, which you decide is 21 metres before the lights. If the lights change before you reach this point you stop; if they change after you have passed this point you continue. You should not approach lights at more than 30 mph, unless you have just seen them turn green and you know this particular set of lights gives lots of time, 20 mph would be better.

Stopping distances

Speed (mph)	Feet	Metres
20	40	12
30	70	21
40	120	36

If, like many people, you feel unable to judge distances, you could use time as an alternative. Most traffic lights take about 1.5 seconds to change from amber to red. As a rule, you could therefore judge that if you can pass the amber light within the next second, you are probably too close to stop safely and should continue. If you are going to take longer to pass the light you should stop.

Whether you use time or distance to help you make your judgement is up to you. What is important is that you approach the traffic lights sensibly and be aware of the dangers. If you approach too fast, or accelerating, or unaware of following traffic, you are asking for trouble. If you approach at a sensible speed and are aware of other drivers, you are in a far better position to judge whether to continue or stop if the lights change.

Lesson 6

Use of fourth gear
Dual carriageways
Braking and deceleration exercises

In this lesson you will go to fourth gear and dual carriageways, where you will be expected to deal with more traffic, and you will be under pressure to do things a little faster in consequence. You will probably not be able to keep up with the speed of other vehicles at this stage, but you will at least get some idea of the pace of everyday traffic.

The most common difficulty at this stage is in being able to slow down properly, particularly if you also need to change down a gear. The exercise in braking and deceleration should help.

By the end of this lesson you should:

1. feel reasonably competent in the use of fourth gear;
2. be aware of the rules applying to dual carriageways.

Using fourth gear

Like the other three gears, you should first concern yourself with the problems of how to use fourth gear and then of when and why. The process of changing up or down should now be fairly familiar to you since it is much the same as with third gear. To discover when and why to use fourth gear you could experiment in the same way as before. Bear in mind while experimenting that it is quite acceptable to stop in third or fourth gear provided there is no manoeuvring involved. It is equally acceptable to change across the gearbox from fourth to second gear, although in my opinion changing down in sequence from fourth to third and third to second will, with practice, give your driving a greater fluency and a greater amount of control, particularly when driving quickly.

Changing up

Accelerate in third gear.
Clutch down.
Off the accelerator.
Change from third to fourth.
Bring the clutch up smoothly.
Put your foot back on the accelerator.

Changing down

Decelerate or brake as required.
Clutch down, while:
Covering brake with right foot.
Change down from fourth to third gear.
Bring the clutch up smoothly again.

In the description of changing down I have implied that you should slow down before changing down. This is not necessarily true. You might also change down in order to maintain speed (e.g. going up a hill) or when accelerating (e.g. while overtaking). In these cases you would keep a little pressure on the accelerator rather than the brake. Once again these situations are best discovered through practice and experimentation.

Dual carriageways

A dual carriageway is a road that is divided along its entire length by some form of barrier that separates traffic moving in opposite directions. This is usually a crash barrier or a fence such as you would find between the carriageways on a motorway, but it could also be a pavement or a strip of grass.

There are usually two or three lanes on either side of a dual carriage-way and as a general rule you should drive in the left lane except when overtaking or turning right.

Speed limits vary. In urban areas the speed limit is 30 mph except where signs indicate otherwise. When the national speed limit signs are displayed the limit is 70 mph.

Dual carriageways are an ideal type of road on which to teach learner drivers to handle a car at higher speeds. There is usually more space than on a single carriageway and therefore, provided the car is kept at a reasonably steady speed and on an accurate course, other drivers will not be obstructed or endangered.

Your first lessons on a dual carriageway should not be too ambitious. Using an urban dual carriageway with a speed restriction of 40–50 mph you can acclimatise yourself to driving on the faster road and to using all your gears by settling at a steady pace in the left hand lane for a mile or so before turning off. The usual problems at the first attempt are in accelerating up through the gears smoothly without wandering out of lane, in keeping at a steady speed, and in decelerating down the gears.

You will have to look further ahead that usual and aim the car at a distant point. Do not grip the wheel tightly. Be aware of, but do not be distracted by, other traffic behind you or passing you in the other lanes.

Braking and Deceleration

One of the greatest difficulties when you start to use higher speeds and gears is in being able to slow down again properly, particularly if you need to change down gears in the process. The usual mistakes are to slow down too late, leaving no time for a proper gear change, or to slow down too early in order to change the gear, much to the confusion of other drivers.

Deceleration is controlled both by gears and brakes, but relies primarily on the ability of the driver to judge how far the car will travel under its own momentum. Obviously a car moving at speed or downhill will travel further than a car going slowly or uphill. Many beginners suffer under the misconception that they have to keep pressing the accelerator all the time if the car is not going to lose power and stall, and also that if they use the brakes firmly the car will come to a very sudden halt. Both fears usually come from the first lesson while learning how to start and stop in first gear, when braking resulted in a jarring stop and decelerating to stop or turn uphill from a low speed may have caused the car to stall. Added to this is the problem that higher gears are still something of a novelty, so a beginner may not realise that each gear decelerates at a different rate. Once these problems are corrected, braking and decelerating may be better co-ordinated with appropriate gear changes. This will take practice, but a lot can be learned from experimenting with the brakes and gears.

1. On a suitable level stretch of road, start off and find out how slowly you can drive in each gear without stalling. For example, in first gear you can drive as far as you like, even slightly uphill, without using the accelerator. It will only stall if you offer resistance by braking or by trying to drive up a steeper hill without acceleration. If you change up the gears you will find that the car will continue to drive without acceleration, but the higher the gear, the easier it will be to stall when resistance is offered.

2. Having discovered how slowly you can drive in each gear, you could then experiment with the deceleration, allowing the car to decelerate, in each gear in turn, from 30 mph to its lowest speed, and noting the variation in the rate of deceleration in each gear and the amount of engine braking offered.

3. Now experiment with the brakes by selecting a higher gear and then slowing from 30 mph to a walking pace as quickly as possible. Release the brakes before the car stops; then change down to second gear and accelerate again.

4. Stop the car from any speed without a bump. Usually this means braking until you are almost stopped, then releasing the brakes as you put the clutch down. Uphill or on the level the car will then roll to a halt. Downhill you will have to keep a light pressure on the brake pedal.

Having now gained some confidence in using brakes and gears, you should try to use your skill to slow down while approaching a junction, slowing at the correct rate and fitting in the gears at the correct speed. You should pay particular attention to the cases where it's necessary to brake and change gear at the same time. The co-ordination and timing involved often gives difficulty, since the brake pedal needs to be held steady and controlled with the right foot while the clutch pedal is pressed down and released with the left foot.

The graph below shows how you might decelerate and fit in the gears from 40 mph in the last 50 metres approaching a junction. Fitting in the third gear at about 30 mph and second gear at about 15 mph means that you can use the optimum engine braking by keeping engine speeds in the

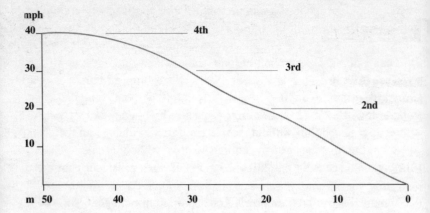

middle of the power band. In this example the engine speeds are falling from about 2500 to 1500 rpm in each gear as the car slows. If you change down at too high or too low a speed the control of the car will suffer because the engine braking will be either excessive or ineffective. You will only be able to select the lower gears at the right time if you listen to the sound of the engine and feel the effect that each gear has on the car.

Lesson 7

Emergency stop
Skidding
Speed limits

By now you should be familiar with the basic exercises, and with the roads that you use to practice on, so you should be able to run through the routine of getting settled down with the minimum of help from your instructor.

In the last lesson you were encouraged to drive a little faster and to keep up with the traffic, so this would be a good time for your instructor to clarify the speed limits so that you keep on the right side of the law.

It is also a good time to think about what to do if somebody steps out in front of your car unexpectedly. The emergency stop is included as part of the driving test, and this requires you to stop quickly and under control. It is unlikely that you will lose control of your car except at speed or in slippery conditions, but your instructor should explain how the most common types of skid are caused and what you should do to deal with them.

By the end of this lesson you should:

1. know the speed limits;
2. know how to stop in an emergency;
3. know in theory how to handle skids.

Emergency stop

Hopefully you will not have to make an emergency stop too often during the course of your driving career, but you certainly should be able to stop the car quickly when necessary. On the driving test you will be required to stop the car promptly and under control, as if in an emergency. The examiner will stop you at the side of the road to explain that, at some time during the next few minutes, he will raise his hand

and say 'Stop', at which signal you are expected to stop the car as quickly as possible without losing control.

This all sounds very dramatic but in practice it is quite straightforward since you are unlikely to be travelling much faster than 20 mph when you are given the signal to stop. Futhermore, the examiner must look around to ensure that it is safe for you to stop quickly, so you needn't worry about other vehicles being involved.

When given the signal: brake quickly and firmly. As a guide, articles left on the back seat should fall to the floor, but the wheels should not lock and skid.

Push the clutch down just before you stop. In a real emergency it might be better to leave the clutch alone. Although this will stall the engine, it also allows you to take full advantage of the engine braking and it makes a skid more controllable.

Apply the handbrake once stationary.

When asked to do so, move off again in the usual way. Make sure you are in first gear and that you look around over *both* shoulders before starting.

When you stop, keep the car in a straight line and keep both hands on the steering wheel. Take your time starting off again. It's common for people to make mistakes by rushing.

Skidding

The main causes of skidding are:
(a) excessive acceleration or braking;
(b) cornering too fast for the conditions.

How well your car grips the road depends on:
(a) the condition of the road surface;
(b) the design and condition of your tyres and suspension.

A skid can be caused by a combination of these factors. Learning to control a skid is a skill in itself. The best advice I can give is that you should attend a skid control course once you pass your driving test. Apart from being a lot of fun it might save your life.

Straight line skid

If you brake too hard, particularly on a wet or slippery surface, the wheels will stop turning but the car will continue sliding forward. You will then have no control over the steering or speed unless you very quickly release and then re-apply pressure on the brake pedal in a pumping action. This will allow the wheels to turn slightly and then to grip the road surface. If they skid again (or preferably, just before they skid again) you repeat the process, so that you bring the car to a halt without skidding. This is called 'cadence braking' and although the process requires you to release the brake several times, you will stop quicker and in a straighter line than would be possible if you allowed the car to continue skidding.

Rear wheel skid

If you corner too quickly, particularly on a slippery surface, the back of the car can slide to one side, being thrown out of line by centrifugal force. The correct thing to do is to keep steering in your intended direction – so if your car skids to the right you will steer to the right; if it skids left, you steer left.

The natural reaction, which should be avoided, is to jump onto the brake, but braking, or even lifting your foot off the accelerator very quickly, is likely to aggravate the skid. The correct action is to ease gently off the accelerator and to steer the car in the same direction as the skid. This will need practice to be done confidently, and any practice in this or any other type of skid must be carried out in a suitable environment such as a skid pan.

Speed limits

Speed limits can be very confusing, particularly when a single limit sometimes covers a wide area, so that broad and narrow streets, busy thoroughfares and quiet suburbs are all subject to the same restriction. At other times you could turn off a wide dual carriageway that is limited to 40 mph, on to a country lane with a limit of 60 mph! The following rules might help to ease the confusion.

1. All roads with street lighting are designated urban or 'built-up' areas and are 30 mph unless otherwise stated. This applies regardless of whether the road is single or dual carriageway.

2. The speed limit can be raised (or lowered) within the built-up area by a sign placed at the roadside displaying the permitted speed.

3. If the national speed limit sign is displayed, the speed limit is 60 mph if the road is a single carriageway and 70 mph if it is a dual carriageway.

4. Outside the urban area (i.e. where there is no street lighting) the national speed limit applies unless a lower speed is displayed.

5. Motorways are governed by different rules and regulations and are all 70 mph unless a lower limit is displayed.

These limits are for cars, light vans and motorcycles. Note: the limits are different if you are towing a trailer or if you are driving a bus or heavy goods vehicle.

Lesson 8

Reversing straight
Reversing around a square corner

As usual you should start with a review of what you have done. Then you can complete your basic knowledge of gears by going to a quiet road where you can be shown how to use reverse.

Reversing around a corner is a test requirement, and in this lesson you will cover the most common variation of it: reversing around a sharp corner to the left.

By the end of this lesson you will therefore:

1. understand how to reverse in a straight line;
2. understand how to reverse around a square corner to the left.

Reversing

The driving test often requires you to reverse your car round a corner to the left and to continue driving backward for a short distance in a straight line. You would be expected to keep reasonably close to the kerb throughout (about 1/2–1 metre, 2–3 feet). An examiner wants to see that you keep the car under adequate control and that you show due regard for other road users.

The driving test requirement should be regarded as a bare minimum. Your aim should be to drive in reverse gear as well and as safely as you would going forward.

The main points about driving in reverse are as follows:

1. When starting and stopping, the controls are used in the same way as going forward except that you select reverse gear instead of first.

2. The steering wheel is also turned in the same direction as going forward and the same pull-push technique is used to turn corners,

although you may hold the wheel with one hand when driving back in a straight line if you prefer. By resting your other hand on the back of the seat you will be better able to turn around to see where you're going.

3. You may remove the seat belt if you wish.

4. You should look around to see where you are going. Do not try to reverse by using your mirrors. Be especially watchful of children, who may be out of sight behind the car.

5. You must not reverse a greater distance than necessary.

6. You have no priority over any vehicle while going backward. Do not reverse if it is likely to endanger or inconvenience any other road user.

7. Indicators are not normally required when going backward but on most cars the reversing lights come on automatically when you select reverse gear.

8. You must not reverse from a side road or an entrance into a main road.

For your first exercise you should find a quiet road and practise reversing back in a straight line, keeping parallel to the kerb. Keep the speed strictly under control and be prepared to stop at any time if you lose control of the steering or if any other traffic turns into the road.

Driving in reverse can be disorientating, and at first it is easy to turn the wheel in the wrong direction by mistake.

The car also responds differently because the front wheels are doing the steering by swivelling the car around the back wheels.

To overcome these problems you should note where the straight line is on the steering wheel and then, while driving back, turn the wheels slightly to the right and straighten up again, and then turn slightly to the left and straighten up again. Provided you never lose track of where the straight line is on the steering you should begin to feel that you have some control over the way the car is heading. Once you feel that you can aim the car in the right direction, try to reverse from a straight line near to the kerb, out around a parked car and back to the pavement again. This exercise is good preparation for parallel parking so try to finish up neatly with your wheels close and parallel to the kerb.

Reversing around a square corner

Reversing around a right angled corner is always easier from a teaching point of view because, unlike bends which curve around at different rates, a square is always the same. This means that you can use the same formula to reverse into a parking space, a garage, or a side road. I will deal with reversing around curves in lesson 11.

You should stop the car about two car lengths past the corner and about 60 cm (2 feet) from the kerb. You then reverse around the corner and continue along the side road for a short distance, keeping the car reasonably close to the kerb throughout and without causing inconvenience to any other road user. You will find the exercise easier to cope with at first if you break it down into three parts.

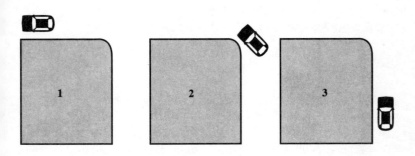

1. Stop on the major road with your wheels straight and your car parallel to the kerb. Reverse until the straight edge of the pavement (down the side road) is lined up visually with a point on the side window directly above the rear wheel. Stop.

2. When you start off again, move the car as slowly as possible while turning the steering to the left as far and as quickly as possible. Wait until your car is almost parallel to the side road. Stop.

3. Move back again very slowly but this time turn the wheel back to the right the same amount as you did to the left (usually about two turns) so

that the wheels come straight as the car comes fully parallel to the side road. Reverse a short distance in a straight line and stop.

Throughout the exercise watch out for other drivers or pedestrians and be prepared to stop or to move forward again if necessary. Be particularly careful as you turn into the side road because the front of the car will swing out as you turn. You should look both ways along the road before you continue.

Lesson 9

Congested streets
Pelican crossings
Reversing to the right

Once you've revised what you've learnt you can add a busier road to your route, where the traffic is slow moving and congested. The skills involved in driving along congested streets are no different from those used on quiet roads, except that you will have to start and stop more frequently, position more accurately, and generally fit in with the traffic. Driving on busier streets for the first time can be a nerve-wracking experience, and it is often a good idea to drive along the same street two or three times to familiarise yourself with the problems and surroundings, retreating to the quieter roads each time so that you can take your mind off the traffic and concentrate on the manoeuvres.

These include reversing around the corner to the right, which is included in this lesson.

How to deal with the other type of pedestrian crossing, the pelican crossing, is also included.

By the end of this lesson you should:

1. be familiar with the problems and features of a typical congested street;
2. be able to reverse into an opening on the right;
3. know how to handle a pelican crossing.

Congested streets

For your initial exercises you worked in quiet residential streets so that you could concentrate on learning basic car control without distraction from other traffic. With the introduction to driving on dual carriageways and in traffic you were put under a bit of pressure from other drivers to do things a little faster.

On congested streets the pressures are even greater. With cars, buses, lorries and pedestrians all vying for space as they go about their business, there is a lot of stopping, starting, and manoeuvring going on. The greatest problem for a beginner is in being able to control the car in this environment, reacting as necessary, without being distracted.

As with all other exercises, the objectives while driving in a busy area should be clear and in line with your skill.

Therefore, on the first trips through a congested area you are more likely to be concentrating on keeping control of the car than to be trying to fit in with the traffic, but you should use these first experiences to familiarise yourself with the features and problems most commonly associated with such areas.

The most common features would include, for example pelican crossings, bus lanes and box junctions, for which there are standard rules in the 'Highway Code'.

The most common difficulties are those presented by the traffic – for example, pedestrians crossing, buses stopping, vehicles parking or other cars pushing into the traffic from side streets.

You will probably feel unready to cope at this stage but having been presented with the problems, the techniques of changing lanes, of putting continuity into stopping and starting, and of keeping with the traffic flow, all of which are covered in the subsequent lessons, will have more meaning and poignancy.

Having carried out these lessons you will find that driving in a congested area is no more difficult that driving elsewhere. You just need to keep a cool head and anticipate how the traffic is moving so that you can fit in without feeling rushed.

Pelican crossings

A pelican crossing is a pedestrian crossing controlled by traffic lights. The lights are activated by a pedestrian pressing a button at the roadside – hence the name. Pelican is a word formed by shortening the words 'pedestrian light control'. From a driver's point of view the main points are as follows.

1. As with any traffic light you should check your mirror on approach and be prepared to slow down or stop if the lights change to red.

2. Unlike the zebra crossing you would not stop for pedestrians waiting at the roadside unless the lights are red.

3. When the lights show red you are obliged to stop. They will stay on red for only a few seconds (usually seven seconds) before changing to flashing amber.

4. When the lights are flashing amber you must give way to pedestrians who have started to cross the road, but not to those at the roadside who have not yet started to cross. The lights will stay flashing amber for a further seven seconds before changing to green.

5. If the road is clear you may continue when the light is flashing amber or when it is green.

6. As with zebra crossings you must not overtake or park on the approaches to the crossing (marked with zig-zag lines).

Reversing into an opening on the right

When you are asked on the test to reverse around a corner it will normally be into an opening on the left. However, you can be asked to reverse into a road on the right instead, especially when you are driving something where vision is restricted, such as a van. You don't need to practice this as much as the reverse to the left, but you should include it occasionally just in case.

The manoeuvre is basically the same as the reverse to the left, but a little easier because you can look out of the side window and see where the kerb is. The main difference is that you start just before a side road on the opposite side. When you have checked that nobody is coming you move across to the other side, a couple of car lengths beyond the corner and 60 cm from the kerb as before. After that you continue in the same way as for the left reverse, only this time taking advantage of the view to your side.

Take care to look for other vehicles and give way to them. Remember, after the reverse is complete you must move back to the other side of the road before you can continue.

Lesson 10

Turn in the road
Mini-roundabouts

After the normal practice session you should spend most of this lesson on another one of the required manoeuvres: the turn in the road.

To complete your knowledge of basic junctions, you should also include a mini-roundabout in your route so that you can see how they vary from major roundabouts.

By the end of this lesson you should therefore:

1. feel that you understand how to turn the car in the road;
2. understand the rules concerning mini-roundabouts.

Turn in the road

You may be asked on your driving test to turn the car around in the road using forward and reverse gears as necessary and without hitting the kerb on either side of the road. Although this manoeuvre is commonly known as a 'three-point-turn' do not fall into the trap of thinking that you must turn the car around in three moves. Some roads are so narrow as to require several backward and forward movements to turn around. What you are demonstrating on the test is that you have sufficient control over your car to manoeuvre safely within a confined space.

The basic moves are as follows.

1. Stop in a safe and convenient position on the left.
2. Having checked that the road is clear, move slowly forward while at the same time steering to the right as fully and as quickly as possible.
3. Just before reaching the kerb turn the wheels to the left as far as possible before you stop.
4. Reverse back, still steering to the left; then turn the wheel to the right and stop before you hit the kerb.

5. Drive forward to the right and stop neatly by the pavement. Apply the handbrake each time you stop, and keep watching out for other drivers, cyclists and pedestrians.

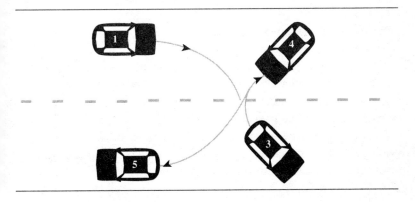

The exercise is fairly simple in theory but in practice most beginners find difficulty keeping the speed of the car under control while steering, particularly if the road surface is uneven.

As an exercise, practise driving forward and backward along the side of the road in a straight line at an absolute snail's pace. Start with no pressure at all on the accelerator and then, when the car is moving slowly, increase the engine speed – but without increasing car speed. This requires a fair amount of clutch control to be done successfully and is best carried out on level ground. Once you have grasped the basic idea of altering the power independently of the speed you should be able to add in the steering and turn the car around – but still at a snail's pace. It will take quite a bit of practice before you can carry out the turn in the road easily and quickly.

Again, once you gain reasonable control over the car, more thought should be put into manoeuvring with consideration for others.

–   Do not turn the car where it might endanger or inconvenience other road users.

–   Complete your turn reasonably quickly so as not to block the road any more than necessary.

–   Keep watching out for other road users throughout the manoeuvre.

Some drivers may be prepared to stop and wait until you finish, but others may not, particularly if you are being unduly hesitant.

From the other point of view you should be prepared to stop and wait if you come across another driver making a turn. Stop well back unless they wave you forward.

Mini-roundabouts

The 'Highway Code' says of mini-roundabouts that you should follow the same rules as you would at ordinary roundabouts, but while these rules can be applied successfully on many small roundabouts there are many more when they would be unsuitable.

This is particularly true of converted T-junctions or crossroads where priorities have been altered by putting two or more mini-roundabouts close together to ease the traffic flow. Even when the conversion involves only one mini-roundabout it is often best to indicate and position as you would at a crossroads but give priority to the right as you would at a roundabout.

In the diagram, for example, the roundabout used to be a crossroads

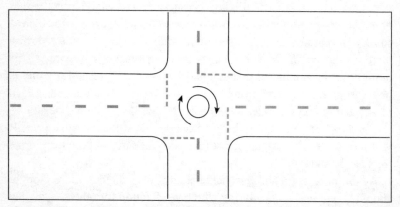

with priorities defined by having Give Way lines across the minor road in the usual way.

The mini-roundabout has been created by simply placing dotted lines across the original major road and by painting a white disc in the centre of the crossroads. Apart from the additional markings the junction has not been structurally altered in any way, so from a driver's point of view the junction is still a crossroads and should therefore be treated as such in all respects apart from the priorities, which are now those of a round-about.

In other words a driver approaching the roundabout with the intention of turning right would hold as straight a course as possible to the edge of the central disc before turning. Try not to drive over the disc, though you can if you need to. As with a crossroads the driver would avoid any unnecessary movement to the left for fear of colliding with another driver in the left lane going straight ahead or to the left.

A simple right turn indicator on approach would be sufficient since the junction is still basically a crossroads. Using a left turn indicator before leaving the roundabout would be unnecessary and possibly misleading. By the same token a driver going straight ahead would not indicate at all and a driver going left would indicate left as normal.

In fact the only difference between approaching a mini-roundabout and a crossroads would be that drivers approaching from any direction would give priority to vehicles coming around the roundabout from their right.

It has to be said, however, that roundabouts come in many shapes and sizes and as a driver you need to use your own discretion. If you feel that at a particular roundabout a variation in positioning or signalling would be helpful or would give better warning to others, then you should do as you think most sensible and appropriate.

Lesson 11

Parallel parking
Reversing around curves

This lesson should complete all the necessary introductions to elementary driving. Start by reviewing and practising all the skills learnt in the previous lessons, including the turn in the road and the reverse around a square corner.

You can then work on the last manoeuvre: parallel parking. This is the newest required manoeuvre; it's also the hardest and the most useful in real life driving.

You can also complete reversing around the corner with some practice of reversing around curves.

By the end of this lesson you should:

1. feel you know how to reverse into a parking space;
2. be able to handle reversing around all kinds of corners;
3. have a general understanding of the basic rules, procedures and techniques of driving.

Parallel parking

Driving forward into a parking space at the side of the road is fairly

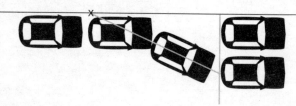

simple and, with a bit of practice, you can stop accurately positioned close to the pavement, but you do need a reasonably large space. If you want to park parallel to the pavement in a smaller space between two parked cars you will need to reverse into the gap. You could possibly squeeze in a gap not much longer than the length of your car but it might make it difficult for the other vehicles to get out. So, unless you want to come back to find your car damaged, you need a minimum space of one and a half car lengths.

1. Drive past the space and stop at least 1 metre (3 feet) from, and parallel to, the parked car on the left.

2. Reverse back until the back of your car is level with the back of the parked car. Stop and check that the road is clear for you to turn.

3. Turn to the left as you drive back, aiming for a point on the kerb beside the parked car behind. This angle is crucial. If you turn too much you will hit the pavement, too little and you will end up wide of the kerb.

4. As the front of your car comes level with the end of the front car turn fully to the right so that you come parallel to the pavement. Stop before you hit the car behind.

5. Drive forward and position halfway between the two cars with your wheels straight and parallel to the kerb.

As with any other manoeuvre you must keep the speed of the car under control and keep watching out for other drivers or pedestrians, particularly when you turn into the space because the front of the car will swing out as you turn.

This manoeuvre is actually a lot easier than most people think. Usually the hardest part is finding a parking space in the first place!

Parallel parking is now a test requirement. You could be asked to do it instead of the turn in the road or the reverse around a corner. For test purposes you are not asked to park between cars. Rather, you are asked to stop beside a parked car, and from that position reverse back to park at the pavement within about two car lengths. This is a lot easier, of course, because you are not so restricted. There is no parked car behind you but you would still carry out the manoeuvre in the same way.

Reversing around a curved corner

Find a quiet corner that curves around gently. Stop the car about two car lengths past the corner and about 60 cm (2 feet) from the kerb. Then reverse around the corner and along the side road for a short distance, keeping the car parallel to the kerb throughout. Make sure that you do not endanger or inconvenience any other road user while you carry out the exercise.

As with the straight reverse, the success of this exercise depends on your ability to keep the speed of the car strictly under control. If you can stop, start and move the car very slowly as required, the steering will come quite easily. At first, however, you might find the exercise more manageable if you take it in stages.

1. If the road is clear, reverse back slowly until the kerb disappears from view out of the rear window. Stop and check that the road is still clear.

2. When you start off again, turn the wheel quickly half a turn or so to the left and hold it steady in this position so that the car follows a constant curve to the left. Wait until the kerb reappears in the back window. Stop again.

3. Your car should now be almost parallel to the road you are backing into so this time when you start off you should turn the wheels the same half turn or so to the right to bring them straight. Continue reversing slowly for a short distance and stop.

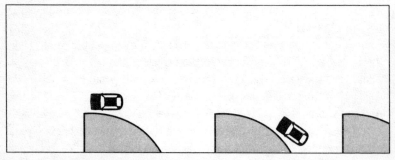

It's unlikely that your first attempts will be accurate, particularly if you follow these guidelines too rigidly! Different corners will curve around at different rates so it would be impossible to give a set formula to follow exactly. These guidelines set out to demonstrate three things.

1. If you turn the wheel a set amount and hold it steady, the car will curve in a constant arc which can then be adjusted to follow the line of the kerb.

2. If you know how much you have turned to the left, the straight line can then be found by turning the same amount to the right.

3. If you plan to stop each time before turning the wheel you will be less likely to lose control of the speed and you will have time to look around for other traffic.

As with the square corner, you should occasionally try a reverse around a curve to the right, in case you are asked to do that on the test instead of the more usual reverse to the left.

Lesson 12

Mirrors
Changing lanes
Dual carriageway – turning right

The first eleven lessons form a framework on which to base your driving ability. The next ten aim to develop your skills by introducing you to a variety of common road and traffic situations and by providing practical techniques to cope with them.

In this lesson you will look more closely at the use of mirrors and will then deal with the everyday problems of lane changing and turning right on a dual carriageway.

This lesson, like the others, is best organised by mixing practice with progress; so for example, you might start on quiet roads, progressing to the dual carriageway for the lane changing exercise, then back on to quiet roads for some more practice on the manoeuvres, and then back to the dual carriageway again.

You should not spend more than 15–20 minutes at a time on each section.

Mirrors

For the first few lessons you will have been concentrating heavily on controlling the car, discovering how to start and stop, change gears, and steer reasonably accurately. You will probably have been aware of following traffic – many people find it very distracting at this stage – but it is unlikely that you will have been reacting to it properly. Without having full control over the car, any checks in the mirror are more procedural than purposeful.

A driver under full control will ideally fit in with the other vehicles, to a large extent driving at the same speed and along the same path as the traffic ahead. By doing this, each driver can watch the road ahead while at the same time anticipating the moves of the other drivers by noting any changes in their speed or direction.

As a beginner, this is difficult to do if you are struggling for control over the car. You certainly won't be able to keep up with the traffic flow, so you will be treated as an obstruction by other drivers. It will be hard for them to anticipate your movements and just as hard for you to anticipate theirs.

As you gain control and start to fit in with the traffic you will be better able to use your mirrors effectively. Because you will be thinking less about basic control you can be more aware of things going on around you and can react accordingly. Sometimes you will have to react to the other drivers but at other times you will have to watch them to make sure they have time to react to you.

For example, if you had to stop at a zebra crossing or traffic lights, you would not stop so suddenly that a driver behind is taken by surprise and forced to also brake heavily. If you are turning right or left, you would give a signal early enough for the following car to react, but not so early as to be confusing. In both cases you need to be watching to make sure the driver behind has time to react and that your intention is clearly understood.

On the other hand you might have to react to the traffic behind instead of them reacting to you. For example, if you are driving in the left hand lane of a busy dual carriageway and see an obstruction ahead, you should be able to change lanes without disrupting the traffic flow. This can only be done safely if you can match your speed and position to an appropriate space in the overtaking traffic.

The main difficulty in using your mirror, then, is not so much in being aware of the traffic as in being able to control your car well enough to act upon what you see. The next few lessons introduce you to a variety of traffic situations. In each of them you will need to be aware of the road ahead and the traffic around you, but you will always find it much easier to react quickly and correctly to the situation if you can use your control and speed to fit in safely with the traffic flow.

Changing lanes

When the traffic is light, changing from one lane to another is a relatively simple exercise. When moving from left to right check your driving mirror and offside door mirror, indicate to the right, and if the lane is clear move smoothly across to the right. To move back to the left hand lane, check your driving mirror and nearside door mirror. Take a quick glance sideways and move smoothly back to the left.

In busy or fast-moving traffic, changing lanes can be a much more difficult and dangerous exercise, particularly if it is done wrong. You have a choice of two actions, either one of which might be appropriate, depending on the circumstances. The simplest action is to slow down or stop. For example if a bus stops in front of you and there is a lot of traffic passing in the right hand lane, all you have to do is wait behind the bus until a suitable gap appears in the traffic, or until the bus moves off again.

On the other hand you might be driving along in the left lane of a busy and fast moving three lane carriageway and have the problem of moving across two lanes of fast traffic to turn right up ahead. This is a much more difficult situation, and the correct thing to do is to speed up until you are driving at the same speed as the drivers in the overtaking lane, position yourself opposite a gap, signal to the right, and then move across.

Many beginners complain that they find it difficult to judge the speed and distance of the car behind, particularly when looking in the door mirror which is usually convex. In fact, it is much more important to focus on the driver in front.

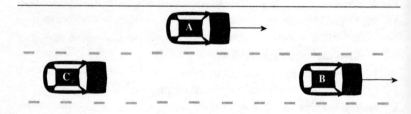

In the diagram, for example, you are the driver of car 'A' in the left lane, travelling at 40 mph. To change lanes safely you will need to match your speed to car 'B' who is overtaking at 50 mph. Car 'C', unless also manoeuvring, must also be driving at 50 mph in order to keep a safe distance, so providing you position your car correctly and signal clearly the driver of car 'C' will be able to ease off slightly, allowing you to move across safely. This, of course, would be difficult to do if your speed or position was incorrect.

This manoeuvre requires a certain amount of confidence to be done safely. If you are unsure of your ability you should look for alternatives. For example, if the right turn you want is at a crossroads controlled by traffic lights, you could turn left instead and then turn around in the side road and come back across the lights. There is no shame in taking a safe option; but for the purposes of this lesson, if such an option has to be taken, you should stop, think about what went wrong and then try again.

Dual carriageways – turning right

If your exercise in lane changing involves taking a right turn off a dual carriageway, the rules are slightly different to turning right on to or off a single carriageway.

A right turn out of a minor road on to a dual carriageway can be done in two halves, stopping on the central reservation if necessary, whereas a right turn on to a single carriageway should be completed in one move- ment, without stopping in the middle of the road. When stopping in the middle of the dual carriageway you need to be careful that you position correctly, and that your car is not protruding into the traffic at the front or at the back. If there is not enough room in the central reservation then you must wait for gaps in both directions and cross in one go, as on a single carriageway.

A right turn off a dual carriageway in to a minor road is almost the same as a right turn off a single carriageway. You approach the turn along the right hand lane of the dual carriageway, turn into the gap in the central reservation, wait for any oncoming traffic to pass, and turn when you think it is safe. The main difference is that, whereas on a

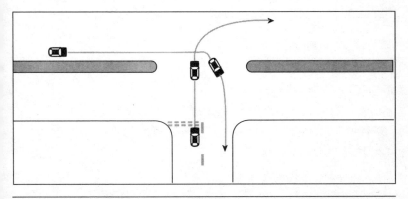

single carriageway you would wait in a position parallel to the centre of the road before turning, on a dual carriageway you can angle the car across the central reservation.

Lesson 13

Signals
Continuous stop/start

You have been using your indicators for some time, but in this lesson you will look at them more closely, together with other signals. You will also deal with another everyday problem: stopping in such a way that you are able to start off again immediately. Like the lane changing in the last lesson, this will help you to fit in safely with other traffic, and to make more effective use of your mirrors and signals.

After settling down, try the stop/start exercise. Then spend a little time on the dual carriageway, practising what you learnt in the last lesson. Later you could go on to some congested streets for a more practical application of the continuous stop/start.

Vary what you do, and leave plenty of time for discussion and explanation.

Signals

The Highway Code says that you should signal to help warn other road users and that you should look out for signals given by other vehicles and take appropriate action.

This sounds straightforward enough, but signals can be as confusing as they are helpful if they are used incorrectly. As a driver you could 'officially' use indicators, hazard warning flashers, headlights, brake lights, reversing lights, or arm signals to make your intentions understood.

You could also use a whole range of 'unofficial' signals, many of which may be useful as long as they are understood by all concerned; and several others which are well understood, not so useful, and best ignored!

Indicators

The most commonly used signals, they warn other road users that you intend turning or moving right or left. The most important points about using indicators are these.

1. Check your mirror before signalling. This is not just a meaningless procedure. Your signal will be acted upon by other drivers, so you can best decide when to signal by knowing what is happening around you.

2. Make sure you signal in the correct direction. On some cars the indicator stalk will be on the right and on others it will be on the left, but it will always move in the same direction as the steering wheel.

3. Once you have signalled, make sure the indicator has been seen and understood by the other traffic. A badly timed or ambiguous signal may not get the reaction you expect.

4. Make sure the indicators stay on until you have completed the manoeuvre, and then check that they are switched off. On most cars this will happen automatically once you straighten up.

5. Make sure you are always watching for signals given by other drivers and acting upon them accordingly. If in doubt, wait until the indicator is backed up by a change of speed or position before acting.

There are other signals that you can use.

Flashing headlights

This has only one official meaning – to warn other road users that you are there. Alternative uses are not advised since the meaning could be misread, but you will commonly see it used as an invitation in traffic when a driver slows down to allow another vehicle to move across or into a traffic stream, or anywhere else where the driver with the right of way wants to let another vehicle go first. It could also mean 'Thank you', 'Hello', 'Get out of the way', or 'Stop', depending on the context.

Arm signals

Since the law now requires all motor vehicles to have working indicators, arm signals are used more by riders of motorcycles, push bikes and horses, than by car drivers. However, you can use them in an emergency if your indicators pack up or, more commonly, to change emphasis on your normal signals. For example, your brake lights warn other drivers that you are slowing down; an accompanying arm signal urges following traffic to slow down as well.

Hazard warning lights

These should normally be used while stationary and causing a temporary obstruction, such as when you have broken down. You can only use your hazard warning lights while on the move to warn following drivers of a hazard or obstruction on a motorway or unrestricted dual carriageway.

Continuous stop/start

In elementary driving you are normally taught to start and stop almost as two separate exercises. When approaching a junction, for example, you would be expected to slow down and stop safely in the correct position; and then having stopped you would take a few moments to gather your thoughts together before remembering to select first gear, and going through the motions of starting off again smoothly.

From an instructional point of view it could hardly be otherwise if you are to learn the correct techniques of stopping and starting without becoming confused.

There are disadvantages however, of which you may already be aware. For example, if you come up behind a queue of traffic which has stopped at a traffic light, you carefully slow to a halt – only to find the traffic moving off again the moment you stop. This familiar situation will have the calmest of learner drivers rushing the necessary actions to start off again, and once you start to rush you will stall the engine, roll back if you are on a slope, or jump forward like a demented kangaroo.

The following exercise will, with a bit of practice, not only overcome this problem, but will improve your foot work generally.

1. Find a stretch of quiet road, preferably with a slope.

2. Start off, driving uphill.

3. Choose a point to stop, such as at a Give Way line, and slow down in the usual way.

4. About a car length before the Give Way line, put your clutch down and let the car roll forward.

5. Select first gear as you roll forward.

6. The car should have just enough momentum to reach the Give Way line. As you feel the car stopping put your foot on the accelerator and find the biting point on the clutch.

7. Hold the car stationary for a few seconds and if the road is clear move off again.

The main difficulties to overcome are as follows.

(a) If the car is still going too fast when you select first gear, you will freewheel over the Give Way line.
(b) If you brake too much the car will stop short.
(c) If you cannot find the biting point at the right time the car will either roll backward or carry on driving forward depending on whether the clutch is above or below the biting point.

Try the same exercise on level ground and downhill. Both should be easier than uphill since you will not require as much clutch control, but you will still need to brake correctly and select first gear at the right speed.

Most people find this technique tricky to master at first, since it requires a fair bit of timing and control, but once you get it right your driving will flow much more smoothly and you will find manoeuvring in traffic much easier.

Lesson 14

Major roads
Matching traffic flow

Having now been introduced to the dual carriageway and having learnt how to change lanes, this lesson allows you to settle down at higher speed for longer periods, so that you can begin to think more for yourself rather than relying on your instructor.

If you begin in a town or city, you start by following a main arterial road out of the city. Turn off into a small town or village where you can take a short break, perhaps practising some manoeuvres. Then drive back.

Since you are following the same main road for much of the time, you will not need your instructor to give you so many directions. You may like to combine this lesson with the next one to make a pleasant two hour run.

Major ('A') roads

If, like many people, your first experience of driving has been in an urban environment, it will come as something of a relief to get away from the restrictions imposed upon you in town, and to experience the 'open road'. Although many primary routes can be as congested as urban roads there are still many places where the way you drive is governed less by the traffic and more by the road conditions.

Most major roads, particularly primary routes, are a mixture of single and dual carriageways. Major junctions, sharp bends and other such hazards are kept to a minimum so that traffic can flow along for mile after mile at a fairly fast and even pace. Unless lower limits are indicated the speed limit is 60 mph on a single carriageway and 70 mph on a dual carriageway.

The way you drive will be familiar, if faster. Keep to the left, particularly if there are two or more lanes of traffic, moving out to the right only when making a right turn or when overtaking. Drive at a pace at which you and your passengers feel comfortable and safe, ideally at the same speed as the main flow of traffic.

By matching your speed to the main flow you can keep a constant and safe distance from the vehicle in front (usually a distance of one metre for every mile per hour, or 2 seconds if you find time easier to judge than distance), and the vehicle behind is better able and more likely to keep a similar safe distance. You need to control your speed carefully, if possible using the accelerator alone, and only using the footbrake when absolutely necessary. This will be made easier by reading the road signs to anticipate changes in conditions early, and by watching the vehicles ahead and behind so as to constantly anticipate their actions.

Matching traffic flow

When you are driving on a clear road with no other traffic, you can 'within limits' drive as fast or slow as you wish. On the other hand, if you are driving on a busy road, it is safest to integrate yourself with the main traffic – where possible accelerating, decelerating and maintaining a steady speed with the traffic. By so doing, each driver can settle into a safe position in relation to the other drivers behind and in front, and can therefore anticipate and react to changes in conditions much more easily. A driver going faster or slower than the main flow will be disruptive and unsettling to other drivers, but this doesn't mean you should exceed the speed limit.

Learner drivers all suffer the same problems to a greater or lesser extent in being unable to start off or accelerate with a queue of traffic. They also have difficulties in keeping a steady speed and slowing down with the traffic. In short, they are often the disrupting or unsettling influence that everybody wants to avoid.

While driving on the open roads you could try an exercise to overcome this problem. Choose a suitable 'target' vehicle – preferably a lorry or similar vehicle which will not accelerate or drive as fast as most cars – and aim to shadow your target for a few miles. You should be able to keep a safe distance without dropping back too far at any point, and you should be able to anticipate your target's every move, so that you can follow steadily and smoothly without breaking any rules.

Once you feel able, try the same exercise with a suitable car – which will be moving faster and will therefore be more difficult to follow.

The exercise sounds simple enough in theory, but in practice the pace of your driving is now being dictated by your target, which means that even if you were driving smoothly at you own pace before, you will now feel that you are being rushed. A slow start, a mistimed gear change, a lack of anticipation, or any other mistake, will be far more noticeable and will often lead to further mistakes as you rush to catch up. Unfortunately, once you get into this vicious circle you can end up totally out of control of the situation. All you can do is slow down or stop, take a deep breath, and try again.

The exercise can be very frustrating, but in practice you will find that your timing and control will improve generally and you will be driving more quickly and smoothly. More importantly, you will be integrating with the traffic, while at the same time anticipating the actions of the others drivers, reading the road ahead, and still feeling in control of the situation.

Lesson 15

Secondary roads
Road signs and markings

For this lesson you want some country roads to practise on, preferably taking you on a circular route. If there are no convenient ones near where you live, take the same road out of town that you did in the last lesson and then take the circle through the country lanes from the small town you visited. You may like to combine the two lessons.

By now (at least, by the end of this lesson) you should be able to follow the signs for your destination. Doing the road sign exercise in this lesson will help you take on the responsibility of reading and acting upon direction and warning signs.

Breaking the exercises into fairly short sections will make the lesson less tiring and more enjoyable, and will leave plenty of time for discussion.

Secondary ('B') roads

Secondary roads are usually much narrower than the main roads, with tighter bends and steeper hills but with much less traffic. Like the major roads you would try to settle down at a reasonable pace that avoids any harsh braking or sudden swerves and, as before, it is best to try and adjust your speed using the accelerator only. Since you will probably be travelling at a slower speed you can make good use of the gears to control the car around bends and up and down hills.

Accurate steering and positioning will help you to drive more smoothly and safely. For example, drive as close as possible to the left on approach to a right hand bend so you will be able to see further through the bend and so that you can take a straighter and safer line.

Good anticipation is also important. Road signs will give warning of permanent hazards such as sharp bends or concealed side roads, but you will not get any warning of pedestrians or animals on the road. You should always be able to stop well within the distance you can see to be clear.

Some roads become so narrow as to be a single track. In other words there is only room for one vehicle at a time on the road. On such roads there are 'passing places' at frequent intervals. If you meet another vehicle, or if a faster vehicle comes up behind, you should stop in a passing place on the left, or opposite one on the right, to allow the other vehicle to pass.

Road signs and markings

The problem with learning road signs from a book (though you must do it for the test) is that it is difficult to place a value on each sign in terms of practical importance to the driver. Only by reading the signs as you drive along can you begin to see which ones need to be acted upon immediately under all circumstances, which need action under some circumstances, and which are for information only.

As an exercise you should drive along a straightforward road for a few miles, reading the signs aloud to your instructor as you drive and acting upon them as necessary. At first this is always easiest on the 'open' roads, particularly on country roads where there is less traffic, because your identification may be slow to begin with, which will not only distract you from watching other traffic, but will also mean that your reaction to the signs will probably be late.

Your instructor may need to prompt or correct you at first, but in time you will not only become familiar with the most common signs; you will also be able to react early enough to fit in with the other traffic, so you can extend the exercise to include busier or more complicated roads.

As a further extension of the same exercise, you might be able to give a brief commentary while you drive along, in which you describe the type of road you are driving on, pointing out any prohibitions, warnings or roadside information, noting the actions of other road users, and taking any action or precaution that you feel necessary.

Most people find this exercise improves and sharpens their concentration and makes them look further ahead. However, it is not an exercise recommended for anybody experiencing difficulty in controlling the car since it will divert attention away from the job of maintaining an accurate course and speed.

A second, and sometimes more difficult, exercise involves reading and following direction signs. This may seem simple enough – the instructor asks you to follow a particular route (e.g. follow the A41 to Watford) and then leaves you to your own devices – but in practice it can be quite tricky, even for a more experienced driver, since it involves watching the road signs and markings, and the surrounding traffic. Particularly in an urban area it is all too easy to find yourself in the wrong lane or taking the wrong road. Changing lanes or direction too quickly could, of course, be dangerous so it should go without saying that it is better to go down the wrong road and turn around than to crash!

Lesson 16

Merging
Accelerating problems
Overtaking

This lesson carries on from the last four in developing your use of speed to fit in with the other traffic, but whereas previously you were trying to maintain a fairly constant speed, this exercise in merging relies on your ability to accelerate quickly. To begin with, you will need to drive to an area where there is a suitable dual carriageway, not only to carry out the exercise but also to give you a chance to settle into your driving.

Before going on to the dual carriageway, your instructor should explain the basic principals of using acceleration and deceleration lanes. Bear in mind there is quite a wide variety of different types of merge on to dual carriageways. Sometimes there is hardly any slip lane and you will have to give way as at a T-junction, and at other times there is a long acceleration lane where you can match your speed to the traffic on the main carriageway. On most dual carriageways you will merge from the left, but there are some where you merge from the right. On most, priority lies with the traffic on the main road, but on some you will merge down an extra lane with equal priority.

How many different types of merge you cover on this lesson will depend on your locality, but you should try to find as many variations as possible. Equally, leaving the dual carriageway might not always be by way of a deceleration lane, and there are many variations on the same theme. Like the previous lessons you could break up the exercise by leaving the dual carriageway at intervals to practise the standard manoeuvres – reversing, parking and turn in the road.

This lesson also includes an introduction to overtaking. It is best to start this on a dual carriageway, where it is easier.

Merging

If you have ever tried to turn out of a side road on to a busy fast-moving dual carriageway, you will know what a potentially dangerous exercise this can be. If you don't speed up quickly enough you will force others to slow down or to hurriedly change lanes. Either course of action could result in an accident.

Many vehicles, such as heavily laden lorries, are not able to speed up quickly. Nor indeed can they slow down so quickly if they are on the main road and someone pulls out in front of them.

To reduce these dangers and to maintain traffic flow at many junctions on fast roads like motorways and dual carriageways, you have to join the main carriageway by driving along an acceleration lane before merging with the traffic in the nearside lane.

The techniques used in merging are very much the same as changing lanes. You match your speed with the traffic on the main carriageway, position behind and to the left of a suitable vehicle, mirror, signal right, and move across into a space between vehicles.

On some dual carriageways you have to merge towards the left, particularly where two major roads join. The technique is the same except that you would use your nearside door mirror and indicate to the left.

If you are on the main carriageway and approaching a merge, you should maintain your speed but check your mirrors in case you need to slow down or change lanes. It might be helpful in many cases to move into the centre lane, leaving more room in the nearside lane for the merging traffic. If that is not possible, then make sure that you have left enough room between yourself and the car ahead for traffic to merge safely.

For the beginner the main difficulty lies in being able to accelerate quickly enough, particularly if the acceleration lane leads away from a roundabout, as is often the case. Initial attempts should therefore be made while joining a road with a speed limit of not more than 40 or 50 mph. You are not allowed on a motorway unless you hold a full licence, but there are plenty of 70 mph dual carriageways on which to practice when you feel more confident in your abilities.

In fact, motorway slip roads are fairly straightforward in comparison to dual carriageways because they normally conform to the standard pattern above, though in some cases the merging lane continues as part of the main carriageway, making it unnecessary to change lanes at all. On the major roads there is a fair amount of variation. In some cases the merge is little more than a re-shaped T-junction and instead of accelerating you will need to stop parallel to the main carriageway and wait for a suitable gap in the traffic before proceeding.

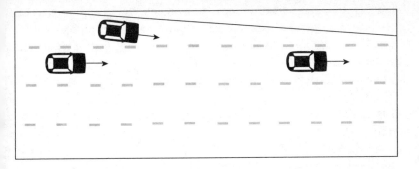

While practising this exercise in merging try to find as many variations as possible so that you fully understand the rules, problems and dangers.

Acceleration problems

Inability to accelerate quickly is a common problem for beginners. Usually the effect of this will become apparent to you for the first time when moving away from the side of the road or when emerging from a junction. In both cases you may have correctly waited until the road is clear, only to start off so slowly that another vehicle appears and is forced to slow down.

As you can imagine, this is, at best, annoying to the other drivers but, at worst, it could cause an accident if it was allowed to happen on a fast road. Without proper acceleration, changing lanes or fitting in with the traffic on any busy road would be much more difficult; merging on to a motorway or dual carriageway could be dangerous.

The difficulty is not usually one of being afraid of driving at a reasonable speed. It is more often a problem of timing and co-ordinating gear changes and steering, with acceleration.

The following exercises might help the situation.

1. Stop the car on a straight and clear stretch of a fairly busy road and prepare to move off again.

2. Wait for a suitable vehicle to approach from behind.

3. As the vehicle passes you, start off and accelerate as quickly as possible up to the same speed.

If the vehicle is travelling about 30 mph you should be able to match that speed in around five seconds without too much difficulty. First attempts are usually very noisy and rough, but with practice you should be able to time and co-ordinate your movements to produce a smooth and progressive flow of power through the gears.

This exercise can then be developed by including a turn while accelerating.

1. Approach the same road from a side street and stop.

2. Wait for a suitable vehicle to pass and once again try to start off and accelerate up to the same speed.

This is more difficult because you have to steer out of the side street and straighten up while accelerating. You should not try to change gear while turning the steering wheel.

You would not always have to accelerate as quickly as possible, but by doing so in this exercise you will highlight any problems that may have prevented you doing so when necessary in the past.

These could be steering problems:

(a) not aiming wheels accurately in the first place or;
(b) moving the steering unintentionally while changing gear.

They could also be timing problems:

(a) if you move the gear lever to the next higher gear nearly simultaneously with the clutch going down you will make full use of the momentum and make a quicker and smoother gear change;
(b) you will time the gear changes better if you keep your hand on the gear lever while accelerating, particularly if you are making two or three gear changes in quick succession.

Hopefully, by experimenting with the acceleration, you will not only gain more confidence in your abilities generally, but you will also be able to use the skill when necessary to fit with the other traffic safely.

Overtaking

Now that you are driving at higher speeds on faster roads, it will not be very long before you come up behind a slower moving vehicle. You could stay behind it, and sometimes it is safer to do so – you are never under any compulsion to pass another vehicle, though the examiner would not be very happy if you spent too long at 10 mph behind a cyclist – but you would make more comfortable progress if you overtook, particularly if it is a slow-moving lorry or a bus.

Overtaking moving vehicles is an exercise which needs to be done with confidence if it is to be done safely. A dual carriageway is an ideal place to gain confidence, especially if the traffic is light. You will have more space and time to overtake, even if your acceleration is hesitant, and unlike a single carriageway you will not have to worry about oncoming traffic.

Generally, when passing another vehicle you would:

1. move into a position where you can see ahead and behind clearly;

2. look for oncoming vehicles;

3. check ahead for crossroads, zebra crossings, or any other hazard that would make overtaking illegal, improper, or unsafe;

4. check that the vehicle you are passing is not about to move out to the right or turn;

5. check your mirrors;

6. signal to the right;

7. if it's safe, accelerate briskly past;

8. as the vehicle becomes visible in your driving mirror, move back to the left without cutting in sharply.

Normally you would drive on the left and overtake on the right. There are only four exceptions when you can overtake on the left.

1. When the vehicle ahead of you has signalled and positioned to turn right.

2. When there are queues of slow moving traffic and your lane is moving faster than the traffic on your right.

3. When you want to turn left at a junction (assuming there is a queue of slow moving traffic going straight ahead).

4. In a one way street where there is more than one lane of traffic.

Of course, overtaking does not have to involve other moving vehicles at all; nor does it necessarily imply using a lot of speed. Care is also needed when passing a parked car, a horse, or a cyclist.

Parked vehicles

Try to keep at least 1 metre (3 feet) from a parked vehicle as a minimum. The danger is that someone might open their door without looking. You will also be leaving a small margin for safety in case somebody appears unexpectedly from between parked vehicles, causing you to brake or swerve.

Cyclists

You should leave enough room for a cyclist to wobble or fall off. They are a lot more vulnerable and unstable than motorised vehicles.

Horses

Going past any animal needs a lot of care. A horse could be startled by sudden engine noise, so pass slowly and quietly, leaving plenty of space. Do not rev your engine or sound your horn.

Lesson 17

Parking (car parks)

As an alternative to reversing around a corner, it might be useful to find a suitable car park and to reverse into a parking space instead. This uses a similar technique to reversing around a square corner, but requires more accuracy – particularly if you are reversing between two cars!

In fact, if you are reversing into a painted square, other cars are not necessary and it is probably wiser to stay well clear of them. Indeed, if the car park is completely empty it offers more scope for general reversing practice. You could reverse to the right, the left, or straight, but always aiming to get to a particular area of the car park, backwards.

Before you go to the car park, try some manoeuvres in the usual way. You may find that the forgiving environment of an empty car park is the right place to iron out any difficulties.

Parking

Parking in a car park space requires a similar technique to reversing around a square corner, except that it has to be done more accurately. It is therefore a good exercise for a beginner who wants to improve on general reversing skills, as well as being of practical use to any driver.

Generally speaking it is considered better practice to reverse into a parking space and drive out forwards rather than the other way around. This is for the same reason as reversing into a driveway in front of your house. Otherwise, unless you have room to turn, you will be forced to back out into the path of pedestrians and traffic. As with emerging from a side road, you can see more clearly in both directions by driving forward. You are also less likely to inconvenience others because you can drive forward in one movement.

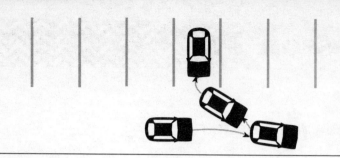

For the purpose of this exercise, it would be most sensible to find a row of empty spaces in a quiet car park so that you can practise the manoeuvre without risking damage to other cars.

1. Stop about a car length past your intended space and about 1 metre (3 feet) from the side, in the same way as you would when reversing around a corner, though in a confined space you may have to turn away from the space to give yourself a head start when you begin to reverse.

2. Drive back until the back wheel of your car is visually in line with the side of the parking space. Stop.

3. Having checked that the front of the car is not likely to swing out and hit anyone, turn fully and quickly to the left. Stop again just before your car comes parallel to the parking space.

4. Drive very slowly back, straightening up the wheels as you come fully parallel to the parking space (usually about two turns to the right). Stop.

Like reversing around a corner, it is vitally important to keep the speed of your car under full control. You should be able to steer very quickly while moving the car very slowly.

Once you feel that you have mastered the technique, you could try to reverse into a space on your right. This is sometimes confusing, although it should be easier since you can see the space more clearly.

If you can reverse fairly confidently into spaces on the left or right, you could have a go at reversing between two cars. You will have to take it very carefully, watching all around and being prepared to stop or pull forward if you get too close to either car.

Meeting other vehicles

On the open road, and particularly on dual carriageways, you will have learnt to watch and respond, to fit in with the traffic flow. To a certain extent this type of response, at speed, is much easier than the responses expected of you in congested streets where you also need to be able to stop and start quickly, change gears, and position the car accurately. The exercises carried out in the next two lessons are commonplace problems that are found in most towns and cities.

Meeting other vehicles in a congested street that is only wide enough in places for one vehicle to pass at a time is a tricky exercise. It requires very good control over your car at low speeds so that you can position it accurately and respond to signals from other drivers reasonably quickly.

Meeting other vehicles

Passing parked cars or other obstructions on a narrow road normally means that you wait until the road is clear of oncoming traffic before you move into the middle or right hand side of the road to pass.

This is reasonably straightforward if there are only one or two parked vehicles; but an increasing problem in overcrowded towns and cities arises from having parked cars all the way down both sides of a narrow street, leaving room for only one vehicle, or line of vehicles to drive down the centre of the road. It is a problem you might come across in the country, on a single track road. If you meet another vehicle, one of you must give way by pulling over into a gap.

In the diagram there are parked cars on both sides of the road, making the safest place to drive the middle of the road. From there you are in the best position to avoid anybody that might walk out from between the cars or suddenly open a car door without looking. You are also better able to see junctions and driveways, and other people are better able to see you.

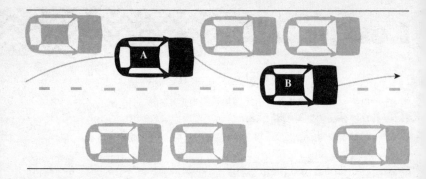

If another car comes towards you, there are two positions where you could safely meet. Position A would be a gap wide enough for you to pull into, allowing the oncoming vehicle to get past. Position B would be opposite a gap wide enough for the oncoming car to pull into.

The theory is fairly straightforward, but in practice manoeuvring in and out of gaps accurately requires quite a lot of skill, particularly if there is a lot of other traffic or you are driving uphill. A combination of the two is not recommended unless you are very confident of your skill in controlling the clutch and steering. Even in light traffic or on level ground, many people find difficulty in positioning the car exactly as they would like without getting too close to the parked cars on one hand and the oncoming traffic on the other.

You need to be particularly careful when turning into or out of a narrow road with parked cars on both sides. Very often you will not be able to see clearly until you almost complete the turn, by which time you could be in a vulnerable position in the middle of the road. In these cases you should try to position your car so that you can not only see further down the road you are turning into, but also so that you are in a position where an oncoming vehicle can get past you, even if that means turning a corner wider than normal. For example, if you are turning right into a congested street you might keep as far to the left as possible, instead of positioning along the centre of the road as would be normal.

Lesson 19

Meeting other vehicles turning right
One way systems

Meeting other vehicles while turning right at a crossroads is an exercise that is often done badly, even by experienced drivers. Partly this is because the rules surrounding the problem are a little vague and often misunderstood. Once again you need to be able to think and act quickly in response to the situation.

One way systems are designed to sort out traffic flow in busy town centres. In fact many of them are badly signposted, and unless you already know where you are going you may have to change lanes at short notice; you may find other drivers doing much the same thing.

Meeting other vehicles turning right

As you are aware, you normally give way to oncoming traffic before making a right turn. This is quite straightforward at a T-junction, but the difficulty is when you meet another vehicle coming towards you which also wants to turn right, as often happens at a crossroads. How should you position in relation to each other?

The rules are a little vague because you have a choice of actions depending on the layout of the junction and the size and position of the oncoming vehicle. In some circumstances you could pass around behind each other in an offside to offside position, and jn other circumstances you could pass in front of each other in a nearside position.

Offside to offside is normally preferable because:

1. neither car is cutting the corner;

2. neither car is cutting in front of the other;

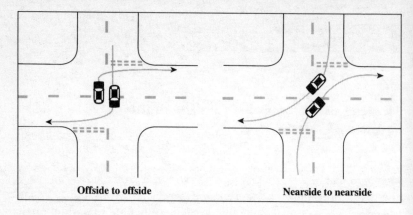

Offside to offside   **Nearside to nearside**

3. it gives both cars a better view of oncoming traffic before turning.

Nearside to nearside is preferable when:

1. the layout of the junction makes this more practical; usually this means the junction is not wide enough for two vehicles to pass behind each other, or it's staggered;

2. the oncoming vehicle is too large to pass behind (e.g. if it is an articulated lorry);

3. there are road markings indicating that you should pass nearside to nearside.

Because either position could be correct depending upon circumstances, right turns at crossroads should be approached very carefully. The layout of the crossroads or the road markings may make positioning clear, but if there is any doubt it is often safer to hang back and wait until you see how the other car positions, before moving forward.

One way systems

Most of the streets in Britain's towns and cities were never designed for the enormous number of vehicles that currently uses them every day. A one way system is a relatively popular way of easing the problem of congestion without widening the existing streets. Instead of having traffic

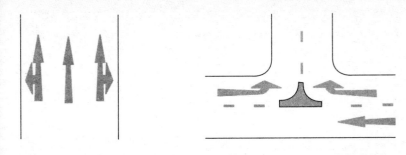

moving in opposite directions, as in normal roads, all traffic in one way streets moves in the same direction.

A one way street is usually divided into lanes. Instead of keeping to the left as you would normally do, you should choose the most appropriate lane. For example, you should probably choose a left lane if you intend turning left or going straight ahead, a right lane if you intend turning right or going straight ahead, and the centre lane, if there is one, if

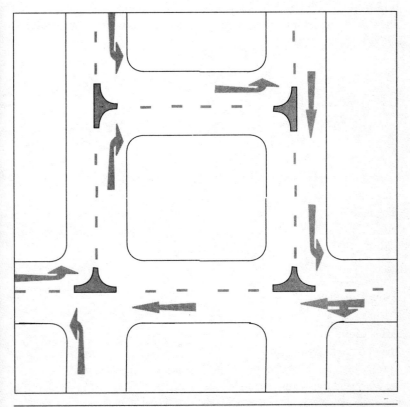

you are continuing straight ahead. The most appropriate lane would vary from one street to another, so you must watch out for road signs, or markings on the road surface.

Unlike normal streets, overtaking is permitted on both sides so more care is needed when changing from one lane to another. Make full use of both door mirrors and take a quick glance to the side before changing lanes.

Whole areas are often made up of a series of one way streets, making a one way system. At junctions, vehicles from different directions merge in the one way streets, where they can change lanes to go off on their separate routes.

This process of selecting the most appropriate lane and of getting yourself into it in good time is what makes one way systems tricky to negotiate and, as an exercise, you should drive a route through a one way system that includes several junctions where it is necessary to merge with other traffic and to change lanes left and right. You will find that the problems are similar to changing lanes and merging on dual carriageways except that you will need to speed up and slow down more quickly in response to the traffic.

Lesson 20

Map reading

The purpose of this lesson is to decrease your reliance on the instructor and to increase the feeling that you as a driver must take full responsibility for planning your own route.

The format of the lesson is much the same as previously. It divides your time in such a way that you are able to practise the now familiar routine exercises while at the same time learning to cope with a new problem.

The problem is being able to get yourself from one place to another with out receiving instructions. You will be provided with a street map and your instructor simply asks to be driven to a particular street where you can carry out a manoeuvre (turn in the road, reverse, etc). Ideally this should be the only instruction. The rest is up to you. You plan the route from your street map and then drive the route, following signs and coping with any problems you might meet on the way by yourself.

The instructor is still with you, of course, to show you how to read the map properly, to guide you back on course if you get lost, to make sure you don't crash the car, and to comment on the way you are handling the problem. The difficulties can be varied tremendously, depending on your ability. At first you might be asked to find your way to somewhere only a few streets away, but as you get better you could be asked to find your way through a congested one way system, or to a street in another town, miles away.

Reading maps

This exercise in map reading will help you to think ahead, to think for yourself, and to be decisive when presented with the unexpected. The routes you follow can be very simple or very complicated, so from an instructor's point of view the best way to plan this exercise is to start you with an easy route and to introduce different problems into each subsequent section.

Your instructor should hand you a street map and ask to be taken to a particular destination, where you can carry out a manoeuvre. The following examples show how your instructor could include various difficulties on the most obvious route. You could, of course, choose to drive a less obvious route – the choice is yours – but you might find that your alternative route presents even greater difficulties!

Route 1 takes you to a quiet road where you can do an emergency stop. This might be only two or three streets away. The route may include a couple of right or left turns at T-junctions or crossroads. This is very easy and is designed to settle you into the idea of planning and driving your own route.

Route 2 takes you to a particular junction where you can practise reversing into a side road. This route might include a roundabout and a busy main street where there are many distractions to cope with.

Route 3 goes to a quiet road there you can turn the car around, but the obvious route on the map leads you through a couple of mini-roundabouts. These are not shown on the map, and neither is the one-way system which forces you to deviate off your planned route. You should not be put off by these unexpected problems. Be decisive and follow the road in the correct general direction; then stop when you can do so safely to check the map.

Route 4 takes you to a place where you can practise the parking manoeuvre, but the obvious route takes you a few miles along a fast main road. If your destination is a few miles away it is often best to follow main or local route signs to the general area, and then to stop and consult the map to find the right road.

On each section you should plan where you are going and then drive your planned route as safely as possible. You should not try to read the map while on the move; nor should you be distracted from driving safely by paying excessive attention to street names or road signs. Plan your route in manageable sections and pull over to check your progress every so often, particularly if you think you have taken a wrong turn. If you miss a turn, or come upon it unexpectedly, you should not swerve suddenly or stop without warning. Instead, you should find a place to stop safely to replan your route, or to turn the car around if that is appropriate.

Most people find this exercise quite tricky. It is easy to miss a turn and to find yourself going off in the wrong direction. That is not particularly important. The point of the exercise is to give you an opportunity to take full responsibility for your actions. Planning and driving a route safely without any help from your instructor will give you a great deal more confidence in your own abilities as well as making you more aware of your surroundings.

Lesson 21

Maintenance
Lights

In the last lesson you learnt to take resposibility for your route to your destination. In this one you will learn to take responsibility for your own car's ability to carry you there. This means you must make sure that it is roadworthy and in good condition.

One of your destinations should be a service station, where you can learn how to put petrol in the car. While there you may also learn how to check and replenish the oil and water levels, and how to use a tyre pressure gauge. Alternatively you may prefer to do this at home.

Checking that all the lights are working by switching on and walking around the car has the added benefit of teaching you which switch does what, which will in turn make you feel more comfortable using them.

Maintenance

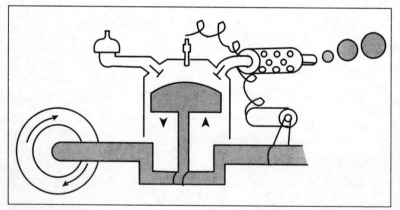

Nobody expects you to be a master mechanic, but you should at least have an understanding of how an engine works and how to carry out simple maintenance jobs, so that your car is less likely to break down in the first place, but if it does you will be able to check for and rectify the most common problems.

I don't think the engine above would get you very far, but it might help you to understand how one works. On an average sized car there are usually four cylinders as opposed to my one.

1. As the piston moves down it draws a mixture of petrol and air into the cylinder.

2. The piston moves back up the cylinder, compressing the mixture.

3. As the piston moves past the top of its stroke the mixture is ignited by the spark plug, causing a small explosion which drives the piston down, turning the crankshaft.

4. As the crankshaft turns, it forces the piston up again, driving the exhaust gases out, and the whole process starts all over again.

Since there are four cylinders working continuously in series, there are a lot of regular checks you will need to make to keep this contraption running.

Petrol

Since petrol is being consumed all the time you will need to keep an eye on the fuel gauge on the dashboard. If you need to fill up, you must know what grade of fuel to put in your car and how to use a petrol pump.

Oil

The engine is made up of a mass of moving parts, centred around the pistons working up and down the cylinders. These need to be kept well lubricated, so you will need to know how to check that your engine has sufficient oil, and how to top it up if necessary.

Water

A lot of heat is generated in the engine and, if your engine is water cooled, you will need to know how to check and top up the water levels.

At the same time you should check the water level in the windscreen washer bottle.

Electrics

Until the engine is running, all electrical appliances, including the starter motor, are powered by the battery. Once the engine is running it generates its own power through the alternator. You therefore need to make sure the battery is topped up and the terminals are free of corrosion. The alternator is driven by the engine and is connected by the fan belt. This needs to be checked for wear and correct tension.

Tyres

You should know how to use the air hose at your local petrol station, or a foot pump and pressure gauge, so that you can check the tyre pressures regularly. Check also for cuts or damage to the tyre wall and that you have sufficient tread (at least 1.6mm over the centre 3/4 of the tyre all the way around). You should also be able to change the wheel.

Warning lights

You should know what all the warning lights mean on the dashboard. Some simply tell you that an electrical device is on and working properly, but others tell you something is wrong. For example, it would be dangerous to continue driving when a warning light is telling you that the brake fluid is low.

Lights

All vehicles must be equipped with adequate lighting – most of it required by law. You must therefore check that your lights are always clean and in good working order.

These lights are at the back of the car.

1. Amber lights – indicators. You should use them to warn other road users of your intentions. While driving along, this is usually to show that

you are turning right or left, but on most cars you can switch on all four indicators simultaneously to warn that you are broken down or stopped in a hazardous position.

2. White lights – reversing lights. On most cars these come on automatically when you select reverse gear.

3. Red lights – often enclosed in the same cluster.
   (a) Side lights – which come on with the front side lights;
   (b) Brake lights – which come on automatically when you press the brake pedal;
   (c) Fog lights – which are high intensity rear lights and may only be used when visibility is less than 100 metres;
   (d) Reflectors – which are not lights at all, but which reflect the lights of other vehicles, making your car more visible at night.

4. Number plate lights – which come on with your side lights, making the back of your car, and particularly your number plate, more visible at night.

These lights are at the front of your car.

1. Indicator lights – which, of course, flash in conjunction with the rear indicators.

2. Side lights and headlights – often enclosed in the same unit.
   (a) Side lights – sometimes referred to as parking lights; these should be switched on when parked on an unlit road at night where you might creating a hazard. You can also use your side lights during twilight or in marginally bad weather conditions to make your car more visible to other drivers, although dipped headlights are usually more effective.
   (b) Dipped headlights. It is advisable to use dipped headlights under any conditions while driving at night to make yourself visible to other drivers. You should also use dipped headlights during the day in fog, heavy rain, snow or at any other time visibility is reduced. Even in clear weather, headlights will make you car more visible, so if in doubt :– switch on!
   (c) Full headlights. On an unlit road at night you should use full head lights so that you can see where you are going, but if another car

approaches you, or if you come up behind another car, you will have to dip your lights or else you will dazzle the other driver. If, on the other hand, you are dazzled by the lights of an oncoming car, the rule is to make sure your own lights are dipped and to slow down or even stop.

Lesson 22

Mock tests
Government driving tests

Having laid down the basic groundwork in the previous lessons by look-ing at the most common difficulties to be overcome whilst driving, this lesson is designed to prepare you for your driving test. This may seem a strange thing to say, since the whole course of lessons is designed to bring you to test standard, but the point is that whereas each lesson is aimed at understanding and overcoming a particular problem, a test is an assessment of your overall competence. A 'mock test' is therefore essen-tial not only to show you the format of the driving test, but also to give you a useful assessment so that you can rectify any faults before being tested formally by a driving examiner.

The lesson format is that you start off by going for a short drive, pos-sibly to the area where you shall be taking your driving test. Having set-tled down, you can then carry out a mock test with your instructor issuing instructions and taking note of your mistakes, but not helping in any other way.

At the end of the mock test you will have gained a good impression of what it feels like to drive under test conditions, and you can work towards eliminating any problems that may have come to light. Some people find that one mock test is sufficient, but most see testing as something that needs to be practised as much as any other exercise. A series of mock tests is therefore a good idea to sharpen up on your skills and to prepare you psychologically on the lead up to the actual driving test.

Mock testing

By this stage you should at least feel that you know what you are try-ing to do, and at best that you could handle the car safely by yourself in any situation. But could you convince a driving examiner of your abilities? The best way to find out is to put yourself to the test, with your instructor acting as examiner.

Government driving tests are very negative affairs. Throughout the test your examiner will issue instructions and expect you to carry them out to the best of your ability, but there will be no comment at all on your driving during the test, and even at the end there will only be brief explanations given of your worst faults if you fail, and perhaps an even briefer word of advice if you pass. After all, examiners and instructors do two very different jobs.

A mock test with your instructor, therefore, needs to be a much more positive affair, so that you benefit from the experience. You could, of course, do much the same as in the examination – drive for half an hour, with your instructor issuing instructions and allowing you to make your mistakes – but for most people this is just a nerve-wracking experience, and at the end of the test you will still only have your major mistakes discussed.

A much more relaxing and enjoyable way of doing mock tests is to divide the time into short sections, starting or finishing each one with a standard exercise, and coping with a different problem during each section. For example:

Section 1:   Start off; carry out a few simple left and right turns to settle down.
Stop.

Section 2:   Emergency stop. Drive a route including a busy shopping street.
Stop.

Section 3:   Turn in the road. Drive a short route including roundabouts and/or mini-roundabouts. Stop.

Section 4:   Reverse around a corner. Then drive a short section of fast road or dual carriageway including a right turn or necessary lane change.
Stop.

Section 5:   Reverse parking. A short drive to get you back to where you started.
Stop. Highway Code questions.

Each section only lasts a few minutes, during which your instructor only issues instructions and allows you to make your mistakes as before, but because each section is fairly short you will be able to discuss all the silly, careless mistakes, as well as major errors, each time you stop.

Your instructor not only comments on your mistakes, but also keeps a tally of how many mistakes you make in each section, and at the end of the test can give you a final score. Ideally you should have no mistakes at all, but realistically you would be doing very well to score less than ten. If you score more than ten, or if any of your mistakes are dangerous (i.e. if your instructor has to intervene) you 'fail' your mock test.

Most people prefer this type of testing because it is more relaxed and more positive. You know exactly where you are making mistakes, so you can eliminate them. You gain confidence in your own abilities and you can take a 'test' as often as you wish, trying to better your previous score each time.

Government driving tests

If you can pass a mock test with your instructor, you are probably ready to take the formal driving test with an examiner. This is a source of great anxiety to many people, but in fact if you can handle a car reasonably competently you should find the test very straightforward.

On the day of the driving test you drive up to the test centre with your instructor and go and sit down in the waiting room. When the examiner comes out, you will be asked to sign an insurance declaration and to produce your driving licence or some other form of identification. On the way out to the car you will be asked to read a number plate to check that your eyesight is up to the required standard. You then get into your car and settle down while the examiner makes a brief check to see that your car is generally roadworthy, that there are no obvious defects, and that your 'L' plates are properly displayed. The examiner then gets into the passenger seat beside you, explains that you should simply follow the road ahead of you unless you are instructed to do otherwise, and that you can start when you are ready. You will then be directed through a short route, which usually takes about half an hour, part of which would be on busier roads where you would be expected to cope with other traffic or pedestrians, and part on quieter roads where you can carry out the required exercises. The type of road you drive on, and the type of junctions or difficulties you encounter, depends on the route chosen by the examiner, so it is helpful if you are familiar with the local area.

Throughout the test the examiner will not offer any help, encouragement, or advice, simply because this may affect your driving. An examiner's job is to try and gain an impression of how you would cope if you were by yourself, by issuing instructions and watching how you carry them out. All the instructions, therefore, are issued clearly and in good time. There is certainly no attempt to trick you or catch you out.

At the end of the test you will finish back outside the test centre, where you will be asked a few questions on the Highway Code and on driving in general. Usually this means identifying about half a dozen road signs and answering two or three questions on any subject the examiner chooses. (From July 1996 this section will be replaced with a separate, written theory test, which you will have to pass before you can do the practical test. Once you pass the theory, you will have two years to pass the practical (and as many tries as you like). If you still haven't passed then you will have to re-sit the theory.)

You will then be told if you have passed or failed. The examiner will give you a pre-printed form with any problems underlined. If you pass you will get another form which you can send off and exchange for a full licence.

Lesson 23

Motorway driving

It is often said that you only really start to learn how to drive after you pass your driving test and, however true that is, there is certainly one area that is not covered in your driving lessons, and that is motorway driving. You're only allowed to drive on a motorway if you hold a full licence.

This lesson therefore assumes that you have passed your test and torn up your 'L' plates. The lesson should begin by making all the checks necessary to ensure that your car is roadworthy and capable of driving at high speeds for long periods. On future trips you may not always think these necessary, and indeed on this occasion you might not be using your instructor's car anyway, but you should still go through the motions to make sure that you know what checks to make and how to make them. You can then start off and follow a route that will not only familiarise you with driving on the motorway, but which also includes as many of the potential problem areas as possible.

A suitable plan would therefore be to join the motorway off a slip road and then to concentrate on fitting in with the main flow of traffic, driving at a settled speed, keeping your distance from other vehicles, overtaking as necessary and generally familiarising yourself with the traffic and the surroundings. You could then leave the motorway after a while to drive into a town centre so as to readjust to the slower pace, perhaps even stopping for a while to rest and discuss any problems.

You could then rejoin the motorway for the return journey, perhaps calling into a service station on route, or changing from one motorway to another if that opportunity arises. You will find that all the basic skills required will be fairly familiar to you, having driven on fast dual carriageways, although some people find the motorway environment off putting and even intimidating at first because of the relentlessly fast-moving traffic and lack of opportunity to escape by turning off or stopping.

By the end of the lesson you should feel: confident of being able to complete a normal journey on the motorway by yourself; that you know how to guard against breaking down on the motorway, and what action to take if you do; and that you understand the dangers that can lead to accidents on the motorway and how to avoid them.

Motorways

Although motorways are dual carriageways like many other primary roads, they are governed by different rules and regulations that affect their construction and use. In construction, a motorway is designed as a continuous road, uninterrupted by sharp bends, steep hills, or any type of junction except slip roads which allow traffic to join or leave the motorway on the left. In theory, a motorway is an arterial road on which a vehicle could travel from one end of the country to the other at a steady 70 mph.

To help this flow, there are also prohibitions affecting its use. Pedestrians, animals, pedal cycles, small motor cycles, invalid carriages, agricultural vehicles, and slow moving vehicles carrying oversize loads, must not use motorways. Surprisingly, learner drivers are also prohibited, although most people would argue that there is a need for more practical instruction on motorways. However, the basic skills required can be learned on any fast dual carriageways before you pass your driving test; the general rules can be read in the Highway Code, and any instructor would be pleased to give you instruction on the motorway after you pass your test.

Before driving on to the motorway, make a thorough inspection of your vehicle, particularly if you are going on a long journey. You should check the oil, water, windscreen wipers and washers, tyres (not forgetting the spare tyre), lights and petrol. Service areas can be a long way apart on a motorway.

Unless you get on the motorway at its beginning, you will join by way of a slip road. Use the acceleration lanes as you would on a dual carriageway, merging into the traffic in the left hand lane without causing inconvenience or danger to other drivers.

Once on the motorway, try to find a speed which fits in with the main flow of traffic. You can be as much of a menace to others if you drive too slowly as you can if you drive too fast. Perhaps the best strategy is to settle to the speed of traffic in the left hand lane. Once you have settled, you should try to maintain a steady speed, moving out to the centre and occasionally the right hand lane to overtake slower moving vehicles that will disrupt your flow. You will find this technique more relaxing and safer, since you are probably driving at the same speed as the majority of other traffic on the motorway, and this in turn means that you can drive for longer periods without feeling tired, although on a long journey it is not advisable to drive for more than a couple of hours at a time before pulling into a service area for a break.

If you are unlucky enough to break down on the motorway, you should pull over on to the hard shoulder, switch on the hazard warning lights, get the passengers out of the car by the doors furthest from the carriageway, and walk to the nearest telephone. These are situated every mile along the motorway and there are marked posts every hundred metres to point you in the right direction. The telephones connect you with the local motorway police who will be able to put you in touch with any service you need to get you going again.

When you leave the motorway, there will be countdown markers leading up to a deceleration lane. You should have positioned yourself in the nearside lane before you reached the first countdown marker so that you don't cut across the traffic at the last moment. Indicate to the left and move into the deceleration lane before slowing down, so as not to disrupt the flow of traffic on the motorway. The deceleration lane will normally lead up to a roundabout. As you approach the roundabout check your speedometer. If you have been driving for a long period at high speed you may be going faster than you think.

Lesson 24

Driving in ice and snow
Driving in rain
Driving in fog

The lessons that I have suggested so far follow a sequence that would have to be rearranged depending on the type of roads or junctions in your locality. Your own lessons can be planned to include or avoid any traffic situation you like depending on your own level of skill. Nobody, however, can plan lessons that include different weather conditions to order, so although you should know how to cope with the various types of weather in theory, and a session should be set aside for this, you can only apply advice practically when conditions allow, doing the rest of the lesson in pieces at various different times.

Whether or not you go out on a driving lesson in bad weather is largely a matter of common sense, but is not always obvious. For example, you might not be deterred when it's raining, but you would certainly think twice about driving in icy conditions, particularly if it's snowing as well. However, going out in these conditions with an instructor for the express purpose of learning about the problems you might face and how to cope with them is a lot more sensible than finding yourself in the same conditions for the first time having passed your test and on your own.

This of course, would not be helpful to someone who has never driven before; nor to someone who has problems controlling the car in the best of conditions!

Driving in ice and snow

Any bad weather condition can make driving difficult, but none more so than ice and snow. In a snow storm it is difficult to see where the road is, let alone where the other drivers are. It is also more difficult to stop, start or turn corners when the road is slippery. Even if you can control your own car, it will not take long to realise that there are a lot of others who cannot!

Most of the problems of reduced visibility refer to driving in snow.

1. Before setting out let the car engine warm up properly. As well as allowing the heater and demisters time to clear the windows, your engine will be more responsive, making the car easier to control.

2. Do not drive away with windows only partly cleared of ice and snow. It is illegal and dangerous. Make sure the lights are clear of snow.

3. Use your windscreen wipers and dipped headlights.

4. It is often difficult in snow to see the edges of the road. Where possible follow the tyre tracks of other vehicles. If there are no tracks, keep midway between hedges or houses, but keep a sharp look out for vehicles coming from the opposite direction.

5. Snow may obliterate road markings. Broaden your field of view to look for gaps in hedges or between houses which may be side roads. Even if you know the road, assume that you must stop at any junction. In icy conditions others might not be able to stop.

6. Falling snow, particularly swirling in your headlights at night, can have a disorientating hypnotic effect. This can be extremely tiring, so keep your journeys short or take frequent breaks.

In icy conditions, the main problems are those of reduced control.

1. Starting off, particularly uphill, the wheels may begin to spin. This is usually caused by using too much power. Take your foot off the accelerator and try to move forward with the engine at tick-over speed. Aim to move forward as slowly as possible and only use the accelerator once you have gained some forward momentum. Even then add power very cautiously.

2. Once moving on icy roads, any acceleration, braking or steering at all can cause the car to slide. The way to cope with this is to expect the car to slide, and turn the wheels to go with it, instead of fighting it. You will then discover that you can control the slide, although your capacity for braking, acceleration and steering is greatly reduced. Any harsh or

sudden movements will reduce control even further so you should make your movements as smooth and as gradual as possible by using your gears to control the speed, in preference to the brakes. Before reaching a bend or hill, get the correct speed and gear in good time. Using your brakes on a bend is very dangerous in slippery conditions.

3. If you do lose control and look as if you are heading for a serious accident, try to use the control you have to reduce the severity of the crash. For example, it is better to drive through a hedge than under an articulated lorry. Both will stop you, but the lorry may stop you more permanently!

Driving in rain

As with most adverse weather conditions the problems of driving in rain are those of reduced visibility and control. It doesn't have to be pelting down with rain before these problems arise. Even a light drizzle can cause the windows to mist over, and make the road slippery. Generally, you should make sure that you can see properly, that you can be seen, and that you take into consideration the fact that your tyres will not have so much grip in the wet.

The main points relating to visibility are these.

1. Use your windscreen wipers.

2. Switch on dipped headlights. Even in light rain it will make you more visible to anyone with misted over windows.

3. Where visibility is seriously reduced (under 100 metres, or 328 feet) use your fog lamps. This is particularly relevant on faster roads or in heavy rain when there might be a lot of spray thrown up by other vehicles.

4. Where spray is concerned keep well away from other vehicles, especially lorries, and resist the temptation to overtake if you cannot see. Even after the rain has stopped spray will be thrown up on to your windscreen, so make sure the windscreen washer bottle is well topped up and

that your headlights are kept clear.

5. Use your heater and demisters, or if necessary keep a window open to keep the windows and windscreen clear.

6. When emerging from a side road, or starting off from the roadside, open your window. You might get wet, but you will also be better able to see and to hear other traffic approaching.

Driving on wet roads will have the same effect over the control of your car as ice, except to a lesser extent.

1. Give yourself more space to accelerate when starting off. A skid caused by over acceleration is easily induced; but the fact that it is just as easily controlled by taking your foot off the accelerator is of little consolation if your wheels spin when you are turning across the path of a fast moving vehicle.

2. Avoid harsh or sudden movements by leaving plenty of space between yourself and other vehicles, by anticipating well ahead, and by using your gears to assist braking.

3. In heavy rain, surface water can build up under the tyres so that you lose contact with the road surface. This is called aquaplaning and the effect is that you lose control over steering and braking. This can be rectified by taking your foot off the accelerator to slow down, and can be avoided by keeping your speed down.

4. Avoid driving through deep puddles. Apart from the danger of aquaplaning, you could throw water up around the engine, causing a short circuit in the electrical system, and the engine will stop. You will also be making a nuisance of yourself by splashing water at pedestrians and other vehicles.

5. If you have to drive through a flood, keep your engine speed high so that water is blown clear of your exhaust system, but slip your clutch so that you keep the speed right down and don't splash water into your engine. Keep to the centre of the road where the water will be shallower. Once through, test your brakes.

Driving in fog

The most obvious problem about driving in fog is that visibility will be impaired to a greater or lesser extent depending on thickness. Control of the car, particularly braking, will also be affected by the damp road surface which always accompanies fog.

The basic points about driving in fog are these.

1. Use dipped headlights, even in misty conditions. Fog is never consistent in its density.

2. Use windscreen wipers and demisters as necessary to keep the windows clear.

3. Use fog lights if visibility is seriously reduced. They should only be used if visibility is less than 100 metres.

4. You would normally anticipate the actions of drivers in front by watching much further ahead than you can see in fog, so your reactions will be slower. Keep your distance and give yourself more time to react.

5. Open your window when emerging from a side road. You will be able to see and hear other vehicles more clearly.

6. White lines along the road are there as a guide. In thick fog, where traffic is reduced to a crawl, following the white lines (always keeping to your side, of course) will keep you clear of pedestrians, cyclists and unlit obstructions, while at the same time keeping you separate from oncoming vehicles.

7. White lines also act as a warning. Signs at the roadside may be difficult to see in thick fog. White lines with longer markings and shorter gaps will warn of a hazard ahead.

8. At road junctions, watch out for vehicles turning or crossing your path, even if you have priority. They may not have seen you and their lights will not always be visible.

Fog is often thought of as the most treacherous weather because it is never consistent in its density. It drifts and swirls around, although the movement is not always apparent. Many accidents happen because, in extreme cases, visibility can be 100 metres one moment and 10 the next – the change taking place without any warning. You can imagine the effect that would have on drivers following each other in a queue of traffic on the motorway, particularly if they were all driving at 70 mph. Each one would naturally brake as they drove into the fog bank, but since the cars ahead are not visible each one would brake at a different rate. . . !

This is an extreme example of how fog could immediately reduce your ability to judge speed and distance to nil, but even at lower speeds and with less dramatic changes in visibility, thick fog would still affect your judgement quite considerably.

You can test your own knowledge of driving and the rules of the road by reading the following questions and deciding which of the three answers are correct. There is only one correct answer to each question.

1. What do double solid white lines along the centre of the road mean? (Rule 84)
   (a) You must not overtake
   (b) You must not cross the line at any time
   (c) You can only cross the lines to turn right or to avoid an obstruction

2. What is the speed limit on a three lane dual carriageway for a car towing a caravan? (Page 53)
   (a) 70 mph
   (b) 60 mph
   (c) The speed limit could vary

3. What lights would you use on a country road at night when meeting other vehicles? (Rule 132)
   (a) Dipped headlights
   (b) Full beam
   (c) Either, depending on circumstances

4. What is the effect of pushing the clutch pedal down while driving on the level?
   (a) The engine will stall
   (b) The car will free-wheel
   (c) The car will stop immediately

5. Which lane would you normally drive in on the motorway?
   (Rule 164)
   (a) Always drive in the left lane
   (b) Drive in the left lane except while overtaking
   (c) Drive in the left lane except when driving fast

6. What does a flashing amber light mean at a pelican crossing?
   (Rule 74)
   (a) Stop
   (b) Give way to pedestrians
   (c) Go

7. What is the sequence of colours at a traffic light? (Rule 54)
   (a) Red, amber, green, amber, red
   (b) Red, red and amber, green, amber, red
   (c) Red, green, amber, red

8. When may you stop on a yellow 'box' junction? (Rule 113)
   (a) While turning left but temporarily obstructed by traffic
   (b) While turning right and waiting for oncoming traffic
   (c) Never

9. When may you drive your car in a bus lane? (Rule 97)
   (a) Outside its period of operation
   (b) During its period of operation
   (c) Never

10. What colour are the reversing lights at the back of the car?
    (a) White
    (b) Red
    (c) Amber

11. Where can white zig-zag lines be found painted on the road?
    (Rule 72)
    (a) At a hospital entrance
    (b) At a school entrance
    (c) Approaching a pedestrian crossing

12. What is the minimum tread depth allowed on a tyre?
    (Road traffic law A2)
    (a) 1.6 mm
    (b) 2.3 mm
    (c) 5 mm

13. What is the shortest stopping distance at 70 mph? (Rule 57)
    (a) 53 metres
    (b) 73 metres
    (c) 96 metres

14. What single feature defines a 'built-up' area? (Rule 54)
    (a) Houses
    (b) Street lighting
    (c) Pedestrians

15. When must you not sound your horn? (Rule 136)
    (a) At 11pm in a built up area
    (b) Where it might alarm other road users
    (c) While stationary and not in danger from a moving vehicle

16. What should you do if dazzled by oncoming headlights? (Rule 132)
    (a) Slow down or stop
    (b) Close your eyes
    (c) Put your headlights on full beam

17. When is it permissible to use your hazard warning flashers?
    (Rule 134)
    (a) When your vehicle is being towed
    (b) When driving a slow moving vehicle
    (c) When stopped and causing an obstruction

18. Which technique is most appropriate when joining a motorway from
    a slip road? (Rule 158)
    (a) Always stop and wait for a suitable gap in the traffic
    (b) Use the acceleration lane to speed up and merge with the traffic
    (c) Drive on regardless, since you have priority

19. What should you do if you skid on an icy surface while braking?
    (a) Release the foot brake
    (b) Pull up the handbrake
    (c) Change down a gear

20. How many feet per second does a car travel at 50 mph?
    (a) 32 fps (9.8 metres per second)
    (b) 45 fps (13.7 metres per second)
    (c) 75 fps (22.9 metres per second)

21. What is a 'clearway'? (Rule 138)
    (a) A road that is clear of traffic
    (b) A road where stopping is prohibited
    (c) A continuous road that is clear of junctions

22. What does a yellow line along the side of the road mean? (Rule 139)
    (a) Waiting restrictions apply
    (b) Loading restrictions apply
    (c) No stopping

23. What is the significance of a pedestrian carrying a white stick with red stripes? (Rule 64)
    (a) The person is blind, but can hear
    (b) The person is deaf, but can see
    (c) The person is deaf and blind

24. When driving in fast moving traffic how much distance should you leave between yourself and the car ahead?
    (a) Approx. one metre for every mph
    (b) Approx. one foot for every mph
    (c) Approx. one car length

25. What are the amber lights at the rear of a vehicle? (Page 56)
    (a) Brake lights
    (b) Indicator lights
    (c) Side lights

26. What do red studs (cat's eyes) along the road illuminate? (Rule 87)
    (a) The left hand edge of the road

(b) The right hand edge of the road

(c) The centre of the road

27. When would you drive in the left hand lane of a three lane dual carriageway? (Rule 95)

(a) Always, except when overtaking or turning right

(b) Only when driving slowly

(c) Only when turning left

28. If you are leaving a roundabout at the second exit (going straight ahead), what signal would you normally give? (Rule 124)

(a) Left indicator on approach to the roundabout

(b) Left indicator as you pass the first exit

(c) Left indicator as you leave the roundabout

29. What lights at the rear of a car warn that the driver is braking? (Rule 56)

(a) Red

(b) White

(c) Amber

30. When is it permissible to stop on the hard shoulder of a motorway? (Rules 180 & 183)

(a) Only in the event of a breakdown or emergency

(b) If you are feeling tired

(c) To answer or make a call on a car telephone

31. When is 'lighting up' time? (Rule 131)

(a) Half an hour before sunset

(b) Sunset

(c) Half an hour after sunset

32. Under which circumstances would you use full beam headlights? (Rule 132)

(a) In thick fog

(b) On an unlit road at night

(c) On a busy main road at night

33. What is the legal limit for drinking and driving?

(Road Traffic Law A4)
(a) 35 microgrammes of alcohol per 100 millilitres of breath
(b) 35 milligrams of alcohol per 100 milligrams of blood
(c) 2 pints of beer

34. To drive straight ahead along a one way street, which lane would you choose? (Rule 96)
(a) The left hand lane always
(b) The right hand lane always
(c) Any convenient lane

35. What should you do if you miss your exit off the motorway? (Rule 163)
(a) Stop on the hard shoulder and reverse back when the road is clear
(b) Find a suitable gap in the central reservation and turn around when the road is clear
(c) Drive on to the next exit from the motorway

36. If you pass a sign warning of a 'ford' ahead, what would you expect to see? (Page 60)
(a) A type of car
(b) A shallow river flowing across the road
(c) A bridge

37. Under which circumstances may you drive without a seat belt? (Road Traffic Law A3)
(a) If you are using your car to make local deliveries
(b) If you are of a size or shape that makes wearing a seat belt restrictive
(c) If you have a medical exemption certificate

38. Which of the following are not allowed on the motorway? (Rule 155)
(a) Heavy goods vehicles
(b) Three wheeled vehicles
(c) Learner dirvers

39. Which of the following are you legally required to do at a zebra crossing? (Rule 71)
(a) Stop for pedestrians waiting on the pavement to cross

(b) Give way to pedestrians on the crossing

(c) Wait until pedestrians have completely crossed the road before continuing

40. When driving in thick fog, which lights should you use? (Rule 58)

(a) Side lights

(b) Dipped headlights

(c) Full headlights

Now identify the following road signs

41. Black diagonal stripe on a white background. (page 58)

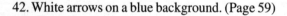

(a) No entry

(b) National speed limit

(c) No parking

42. White arrows on a blue background. (Page 59)

(a) Two way traffic

(b) Pass either side

(c) Road Forks

43. Black motif on a white background in a red triangle. (Page 59)

(a) Two way traffic crosses one way road

(b) Double Bend

(c) Two way traffic straight ahead

44. Red crossbar, white stem, blue background. (Page 62)

    (a) T-junction
    (b) No through road
    (c) Lane closed

45. Black and red car motif (black on the left), white background, red circle. (Page 58)

    (a) No overtaking
    (b) Two way traffic
    (c) Priority over vehicles from opposite
    direction

46. White arrow on a blue background. (Page 59)

    (a) Ahead only
    (b) One-way street
    (c) Single file traffic

47. Black motif, white background, red triangle. (Page 59)

    (a) Road narrows
    (b) End of dual carriageway
    (c) Road forks

48. A pattern of white lights on a dark background. (Page 54)

    (a) Stop
    (b) National speed limit applies
    (c) End of restriction

49. Black motif, white background, red circle. (Page 58)

(a) No cycling
(b) Cycle route
(c) Beware of cyclists

50. A white 'R' on a green background with a yellow border. (Page 61)

(a) Restricted road
(b) Recommended route
(c) Ring road

Answers

1. (c) 2. (b) 3. (a) 4. (b)
5. (b) 6. (b) 7. (b) 8. (b) 9. (a) 10. (a) 11. (c)
12. (a) 13. (c) 14. (b) 15. (c) 16. (a) 17. (c) 18. (b)
19. (a) 20. (c) 21. (b) 22. (a) 23. (c) 24. (a) 25 (b) 26. (a) 27. (a)
28. (b) 29. (a) 30. (a) 31. (b) 32. (b) 33. (a)
34. (c) 35. (c) 36. (b) 37. (c) 38. (c) 39. (b) 40. (b)
41. (b) 42. (b) 43. (a) 44. (b)
45. (a) 46. (a) 47. (b) 48. (c) 49. (a) 50. (c)